Transnationalizing
the Public Sphere

Transnationalizing the Public Sphere

Nancy Fraser et al.

Edited by Kate Nash

polity

Contents

Contributors

Nancy Fraser is Henry A. and Louise Loeb Professor of Philosophy and Politics at the New School for Social Research, New York, and holder of the international research chair in 'Global Justice' at the Collège d'études mondiales, Paris. Her most recent books are *Fortunes of Feminism: From State-Managed Capitalism to Neoliberal Crisis* (Verso, 2013) and *Scales of Justice: Reimagining Political Space in a Globalizing World* (Polity, 2008).

Nick Couldry is Professor of Media, Communications, and Social Theory at the London School of Economics. He is the author or editor of eleven books, including *Ethics of Media* (Palgrave MacMillan, 2013, co-edited with Mirca Madianou and Amit Pinchevski), *Media, Society, World: Social Theory and Digital Media Practice* (Polity, 2012), and *Why Voice Matters: Culture and Politics After Neoliberalism* (Sage, 2010).

Kimberly Hutchings is Professor of International Relations at the London School of Economics. She has published extensively in the fields of international ethics and political theory. Her books include *International Political Theory: Rethinking Ethics in a Global Era* (Sage, 1998), *Time and* World Politics: Thinking the Present (Manchester University Press, 2008), and *Global Ethics: An Introduction* (Polity, 2010).

Fuyuki Kurasawa is Associate Professor of Sociology at York University, Toronto, Co-President of the International Sociological Association's Research Committee on Sociological Theory, and a Faculty Fellow at the Center for Cultural Sociology, Yale University. He is the author of *The Ethnological Imagination: A Cross-Cultural Critique of Modernity* (Minnesota University Press, 2004) and *The Work of Global Justice: Human Rights as Practices* (Cambridge University Press, 2007).

Kate Nash is Professor of Sociology at Goldsmiths, University of London, and Faculty Fellow at the Center for Cultural Sociology, Yale University. Her books include *Contemporary Political Sociology* (2nd edition, Wiley-Blackwell, 2010) and *The Cultural Politics of Human Rights: Comparing the US and UK* (Cambridge University Press, 2009). She is currently writing *The Sociology of Human Rights* (Cambridge University Press, forthcoming).

David Owen is Professor of Social and Political Philosophy at the University of Southampton. He has published nine books, most recently Nietzsche's *Genealogy of Morality* (Acumen, 2007), *Recognition and Power: Axel Honneth and the Tradition of Critical Social Theory* (Cambridge University Press, 2007, co-edited with Bert van den Brink). He is currently working on book manuscripts on migration and political theory and on Nietzschean political theory.

Introduction

Kate Nash

'Public' is a kind of placeholder to allow consideration of the moral dimension of democratic politics. We talk about public interest, public goods, public policy. In each case 'public' is counterposed to 'private', the realm of individual freedom that is increasingly commodified and collapsed into markets. It is also, more controversially, counterposed to the 'private' of domestic space. 'Public' designates an area of social life that is more than markets, institutions, individuals, or organized groups. There are a number of ways of filling the term, but since Kant and Rousseau elaborated the importance of publicity, reason, and the general will in the eighteenth century, the 'public' as the site, the topic, and the outcome of democratic debate has been influential in theory and practice. Since then too, socialist, feminist, anti-colonialist, and anti-racist movements have been working hard to throw suspicion on attempts to define 'equality', 'person', or indeed 'reason' too narrowly when talking about 'public' interest, goods, policy. The ideal of the public sphere, if it is invariably concretized in exclusionary ways, always also gestures beyond itself, to ideals of genuine participation in establishing the common good.

Participation in the public sphere must not only be inclusive and reflexive, it must also be effective. Democratic will formation must at some point be translated into law and policy. Radical suspicion of the public sphere is often pessimistic in this respect: where corporate and conservative lobby groups invariably hold more sway than others when it comes to making decisions that count, the ideal of the public sphere serves to mask domination and exclusion rather than to open up genuine participation. For many radicals the task at hand, then, is not to try to work out what kind of democratic discussion and decision-making could ensure that law and policy are really legitimate, but rather to question the language of legitimacy itself. (Today this is at least as likely to be done in the tradition of Nietzsche, with Foucault and Deleuze, as it is in the name of Marx.) But in any form of social life in which there is integration beyond local, face-to-face encounters, the problem of how to institutionalize decisions cannot be avoided. For radical *democrats*, how to make governing institutions responsive to ordinary people will always be a vital question.

It is a question that becomes all the more complex when we think about globalization. There are undoubtedly global public goods – which are collectively useful or necessary but which markets do not provide: at the very minimum a liveable environment and rights to bodily integrity (not to be killed or tortured, and to be fed and sheltered). And there are global public bads – externalities produced in one country that affect everyone, directly or indirectly (contributing to climate change, to conditions that lead to the collapse of nationally managed economies, to support for international terrorism). Then there are regional or transnational public goods and bads that affect people in areas that cross the borders of different states (war often makes for refugees in a neighbouring country, pollution does not respect state territories). There is a growing network of institutions and organizations of regional and global governance that make public policy and law on a range of transnational issues – the environment, war, migration, human rights, trade and finance. But what are the implications for democracy once it is understood that states, whilst still nominally sovereign, do not independently establish the conditions under which people live within their borders?

Although there is a good deal of interesting political theory now on how global governance must be democratized, the formation of the public sphere beyond the nation-state has received surprisingly little critical attention. Habermas has argued that a global public sphere is absolutely necessary to democratize law- and policy-making where concerns are truly global. For him, however, relatively little is global: he argues that a world organization, whilst performing a vital role as representing world unity, should actually only have the specialized tasks of keeping the peace and guaranteeing human rights (though actually, this is far from minimal) (Habermas 2009: 120). Most political issues related to globalization are transnational; and open, responsive, overlapping, and transparent national and regional (e.g., European) public spheres that enable citizens and governments to learn to become less concerned with defending national interests would be sufficient to negotiate the making of law and policy to regulate cross-border affairs (Habermas 2001, 2009). Habermas is, however, sceptical about whether any of this might be possible today. In contrast, some have argued that the internet enables the possibility of a deliberative 'public of publics' at the global scale (Bohman 2007), and that transnational social movements are actually now achieving a form of global public sphere (Castells 2009; Guidry et al. 2000; Smith 2007). In addition, the idea of global civil society is often used in ways that suggest it is democratic. In such accounts, largely because of the history of the term 'civil society' in the democratization of countries in Eastern Europe and Latin America in the late twentieth century, the activities of left-liberal NGOs (e.g., Friends of the Earth, Human Rights Watch) are treated as legitimate, though their activities do not necessarily involve the participation of those most affected by the solutions they advocate. We will do well, then, to ask whether those theorists who see transnational public spheres as possible, necessary, or already existing are actually talking about the same thing.

What connections do they make between 'global civil society', 'public sphere', and 'democracy'? And do the connections they make, or perhaps assume, stand up to critical scrutiny? What is needed is in-depth consideration from a range of perspectives concerning what 'transnationalizing the public sphere' actually requires, normatively and empirically, and how we might conceptualize it in relation to the democratic deficit of existing political institutions.

Nancy Fraser, whose work has made such an important contribution to debates over the structure of the public sphere in relation to nation-states, has taken up this challenge. In the title essay, 'Transnationalizing the Public Sphere', she carefully and clearly analyses what we might expect from a critical discussion of the concept of 'public sphere' if it is 'scaled up'. As she says, critical theory walks a line between adapting the normative conditions of the public sphere as it was developed in relation to nation-states so that these now correspond to existing globalizing realities, and adapting them in an idealized way that does not give any purchase on historically unfolding possibilities (pp. 9–10, this volume). Fraser clearly lays out what she thinks must be retained of Habermas's conception of the public sphere if it is to be 'scaled up' (noting how he has developed it since *The Structural Transformation of the Public Sphere*) as a result of the debates to which she and others contributed so creatively.

Following Fraser's essay, the other contributors to this volume, in the spirit of critical debate, then raise searching questions about her theoretical premises and arguments. A number of us raise questions about the fundamentals of Habermas's theory of the public sphere. Fraser herself expresses doubts about whether he has really been able to reconcile the limitations of empirical debate in complex societies with ideals of democratic legitimacy (p. 18 and p. 35 n. 12, this volume). Can such a fundamental problem really be bracketed (Nash)? And what if the emergence of the public sphere in modern states that were also imperial is more than a contingent fact? What if the ideal itself is limited by the conditions under which it was created (Hutchings)?

In terms of the aims of critical theory as Fraser has stated them, the contributors raise questions about the empirical claims underpinning her call to reflect on how the public sphere might be 'scaled up'. If practices resembling the public sphere historically enabled the development of critical tools with which to assess 'actually existing' democracy at the national level, does this mean the concept 'public sphere' can be used in a similar way at the global level? It may be premature to give up on local and national publics which, while bounded in space and still linked to national states, need not be bounded in terms of the identities and orientations of those who get involved in or who are addressed by them. Or it may be that, where a global state is unlikely to develop in the near future, and where the desirability of such a development is itself doubtful, it is mistaken to try to 'scale up' at all. Why not consider rather how national and local publics may actually be transnationalizing, especially considering that state capacities remain massively important (Couldry)? Alternatively, we might ask whether organizations that are actually concerned not with democracy at all, but rather with particular issues of global injustice, may nevertheless have a democratizing impact at the global scale. Might NGOs concerned with, say, human rights make institutions of global governance more responsive to people's needs in practice, even though those affected do not participate directly in formulating their demands (Nash)? Finally, is Fraser's idea of the role of subaltern counterpublic spheres perhaps more promising than that of the global public sphere, especially given the prominence of activists who are trying to develop an alternative globalization (Kurasawa)?

In terms of normative theory, Fraser's main innovation in thinking about the transnational public sphere is the idea that, whilst earlier versions of the public sphere simply assumed that it should involve citizens of the nation-state, globalization requires attention to precisely who it is that makes up the relevant political community. Compared to an earlier version of her essay, published in *Theory, Culture & Society* in 2007, in which Fraser took the view that the relevant constituency for global justice was 'all affected', she now argues that it is rather 'all subjected' to structures of governance who should be included in the transnational public sphere.[1] What is at stake in Fraser's change of view, and is it justified? How is the inclusion of some, the 'all subjected', and therefore the exclusion of others, justified in advance of public discussion, when genuine inclusion is one of the tests of its legitimacy (Owen)? And does Fraser's formulation raise other, more subtle, barriers to inclusion? Does it presume similar subjectivity as the basis for democratic debate? Does the idea of a shared space also require a shared narrative of globalization as having brought about a *new* disempowerment that cannot have the same sense for people in postcolonial states, where democratic debate has long been constrained by conditions set elsewhere (Hutchings)?

In the final essay of the volume, Fraser responds to the questions raised by her critics. Coming as they do from a range of disciplines and perspectives, and followed up by Fraser's careful and characteristically precise consideration, the result is that the volume opens up a range of ways of thinking through this question of globalization and democracy.

'Transnationalizing the Public Sphere: On the Legitimacy and Efficacy of Public Opinion in a Post-Westphalian World' was first published in *Theory, Culture & Society* 24(4) (2007), 7–30. We would like to thank Sage and the editors of *Theory, Culture & Society* for permission to republish it here. Since its publication, the article has received a good deal of attention. We hope the rethinking of democracy in an era of globalization to which it was such an important contribution will be further deepened by the critical engagement with Fraser's argument represented in this volume, and by her characteristically engaged and lucid response to her critics.

Note

1 Fraser used 'all affected' as a principle of post-Westphalian frame-setting in the first version of this article printed in *Theory,*

Culture & Society in 2007 (Fraser 2007), and 'all subjected' in the version that is reproduced in *Scales of Justice* (Fraser 2008) and in this volume. In *Scales of Justice* she argues that the 'all-subjected principle' offers a critical standard for assessing the (in)justice of frames that avoids the problems of the 'butterfly effect', the complexity of causal relations in general, raised by the 'all- affected principle' because it specifies the social relation relevant to democracy, the joint subjection to structures of governance (see Fraser 2008: 64–6).

References

Bohman, J. (2007) *Democracy across Borders: From Demos to Demoi*. Cambridge, MA: MIT Press.

Castells, M. (2009) *Communication Power*. Oxford: Oxford University Press.

Fraser, N. (2007) 'Transnationalizing the Public Sphere: On the Legitimacy and Efficacy of Public Opinion in a Post-Westphalian World', *Theory, Culture & Society* 24(4): 7–30.

Fraser, N. (2008) *Scales of Justice: Reimagining Political Space in a Global World*. Cambridge: Polity.

Guidry, J., M.D. Kennedy, and M.N. Zald (eds) (2000) *Globalization and Social Movements: Culture, Power, and the Transnational Public Sphere*. Ann Arbor: University of Michigan Press.

Habermas, J. (2001) 'Why Europe Needs a Constitution', *New Left Review* 11 (Sept.–Oct.): http://newleftreview.org/II/11/jurgen-habermas-why-europe-needs-a-constitution (accessed 4 November 2013).

Habermas, J. (2009) *Europe: The Faltering Project*. Cambridge: Polity.

Smith, J. (2007) *Social Movements for Global Democracy*. Baltimore: Johns Hopkins University Press.

1

Transnationalizing the Public Sphere

On the Legitimacy and Efficacy of Public Opinion in a Post-Westphalian World

Nancy Fraser

It is commonplace nowadays to speak of 'transnational public spheres', 'diasporic public spheres', 'Islamic public spheres', and even an emerging 'global public sphere'. And such talk has a clear point. A growing body of media studies literature is documenting the existence of discursive arenas that overflow the bounds of both nations and states. Numerous scholars in cultural studies are ingeniously mapping the contours of such arenas and the flows of images and signs in and through them.[1] The idea of a 'transnational public sphere' is intuitively plausible, then, and seems to have purchase on social reality.

Nevertheless, this idea raises a problem. The concept of the public sphere was developed not simply to understand communication flows but also to contribute a critical theory of democracy. In that theory, a public sphere is conceived as a space for the communicative generation of public opinion. Insofar as the process is inclusive and fair, publicity is supposed to discredit views that cannot withstand critical scrutiny and to assure the legitimacy of those that do. Thus, it matters who participates and on what terms. In addition, a public sphere is conceived as a vehicle for marshalling public opinion as a political force. Mobilizing the considered sense of civil society, publicity is supposed to hold officials accountable and to assure that the actions of the state express the will of the citizenry. Thus, a public sphere should correlate with a sovereign power. Together, these two ideas – the *normative legitimacy* and *political efficacy* of public opinion – are essential to the concept of the public sphere in critical theory.[2] Without them, the concept loses its critical force and its political point.

Yet these two features are not easily associated with the discursive arenas that we today call 'transnational public spheres'. It is difficult to associate the notion of legitimate public opinion with communicative arenas in which the interlocutors are not fellow members of a political community, with equal rights to participate in political life. And it is hard to associate the notion of efficacious communicative power with discursive spaces that do not correlate with sovereign states. Thus, it is by no means clear what it means today to speak of 'transnational public spheres'. From the perspective of critical theory, at least, the phrase sounds a bit like an oxymoron.

Nevertheless, we should not rush to jettison the notion of a 'transnational public sphere'. Such a notion is indispensable, I think, to those who aim to reconstruct critical theory in the current 'postnational constellation'. But it will not be sufficient merely to refer to such public spheres in a relatively casual commonsense way, as if we already knew what they were. Rather, it will be necessary to return to square one, to problematize public sphere theory – and ultimately to reconstruct its conceptions of the normative legitimacy and political efficacy of communicative power. The trick will be to walk a narrow line between two equally unsatisfactory approaches. On the one hand, one should avoid an empiricist approach that simply adapts the theory to the existing realities, as that approach risks sacrificing its normative force. On the other hand, one should also avoid an externalist approach that invokes ideal theory to condemn social reality, as that approach risks forfeiting critical traction. The alternative, rather, is a critical-theoretical approach that seeks to locate normative standards and emancipatory political possibilities precisely within the historically unfolding constellation.

This project faces a major difficulty, however. At least since its 1962 adumbration by Jürgen Habermas, public-sphere theory has been implicitly informed by a Westphalian political imaginary: it has tacitly assumed the frame of a bounded political community with its own territorial state.[3] The same is true for nearly every subsequent egalitarian critique of public-sphere theory, including those of feminists, multiculturalists, and anti-racists. Only very recently, in fact, have the theory's Westphalian underpinnings been problematized. Only recently, thanks to post-Cold-War geopolitical instabilities, on the one hand, and to the increased salience of transnational phenomena associated with 'globalization', on the other, has it become possible – and necessary – to rethink public-sphere theory in a transnational frame. Yet these same phenomena force us to face the hard question: Is the concept of the public sphere so thoroughly Westphalian in its deep conceptual structure as to be unsalvageable as a critical tool for theorizing the present? Or can the concept be reconstructed to suit a post-Westphalian frame? In the latter case, the task would not simply be to conceptualize transnational public spheres as actually existing institutions. It would rather be to reformulate *the critical theory of the public sphere* in a way that can illuminate the emancipatory possibilities of the present constellation.

In this essay I want to sketch the parameters for such a discussion. I shall be mapping the terrain and posing questions rather than offering definitive answers. But I start with the assumption that public-sphere theory is in principle an important critical-conceptual resource that should be reconstructed rather than jettisoned, if possible. My discussion will proceed in three parts. First, I shall explicate the implicit Westphalian presuppositions of Habermas's public-sphere theory and show that these have persisted in its major feminist, anti-racist, and multicultural critiques. Second, I shall identify several distinct facets of transnationality that problematize both traditional public-sphere theory and its critical counter-theorizations. Finally, I shall propose some strategies whereby public-sphere theorists might begin to respond to these challenges. My overall aim is to repoliticize public sphere theory, which is currently in danger of being depoliticized.

Classical Public-Sphere Theory and Its Radical Critique: Thematizing the Westphalian Frame

Let me begin by recalling some analytic features of public-sphere theory, drawn from the *locus classicus* of all discussions, Jürgen Habermas's *The Structural Transformation of the Public Sphere* (1989). In this early work, Habermas's inquiry proceeded simultaneously on two levels, one empirical and historical, the other ideological-critical and normative. On both levels, the public sphere was conceptualized as coextensive with a bounded political community and a sovereign territorial state, often a nation-state. To be sure, this was not always fully explicit. Tacitly, however, Habermas's account of the public sphere rested on at least six social-theoretical presuppositions, all of which took for granted the Westphalian framing of political space.

1 *Structural Transformation* correlated the public sphere with a modern state apparatus that exercised sovereign power over a bounded territory. Thus, Habermas assumed that public opinion was addressed to a Westphalian state that was capable in principle of regulating its inhabitants' affairs and solving their problems.[4]

2 *Structural Transformation* conceived the participants in public-sphere discussion as fellow members of a bounded political community. Casting the *telos* of their discussions as the articulated general interest of a *demos*, which should be

translated into binding laws, Habermas tacitly identified members of the public with the citizenry of a democratic Westphalian state.[5]

3 *Structural Transformation* conceived a principal *topos* of public-sphere discussion as the proper organization of the political community's economic relations. The latter, in turn, it located in a capitalist market economy that was legally constituted and subject in principle to state regulation. In effect, Habermas assumed that a primary focus of the public's concern was a national economy, contained by a Westphalian state.[6]

4 *Structural Transformation* associated the public sphere with modern media that, in enabling communication across distance, could knit spatially dispersed interlocutors into a public. Tacitly, however, Habermas territorialized publicity by focusing on national media, especially the national press and national broadcasting. Thus, he implicitly assumed a national communications infrastructure, contained by a Westphalian state.[7]

5 *Structural Transformation* took for granted that public-sphere discussion was fully comprehensible and linguistically transparent. Tacitly presupposing a single shared linguistic medium of public communication, Habermas effectively assumed that public debate was conducted in a national language.[8]

6 Finally, *Structural Transformation* traced the cultural origins of the public sphere to the letters and novels of eighteenth- and nineteenth-century print capitalism. It credited those bourgeois genres with creating a new subjective stance, through which private individuals envisioned themselves as members of a public.[9] Thus, Habermas grounded the structure of public-sphere subjectivity in the very same vernacular literary forms that also gave rise to the imagined community of the nation (Anderson 1991).

These six social-theoretical presuppositions tie Habermas's early account of the public sphere to the Westphalian framing of political space. In *Structural Transformation*, publics correlate with modern territorial states and national imaginaries. To be sure, the national aspect went largely unthematized in this work. But its presence there as an implicit subtext betrays a point that Habermas has since made explicit: historically, the rise of modern publicity coincided with the rise of the nation-state, in which the Westphalian territorial state became fused with the imagined community of the nation (Habermas 1998). It may be true, as Habermas (1998) now claims, that present-day democratic states can dispense with national identity as a basis of social integration. But it remains the case that *Structural Transformation*'s conception of publicity had a national subtext. That work's account of the public sphere presupposed a nationally inflected variant of the Westphalian frame.

But that is not all. Thanks to its (national) Westphalian presuppositions, *Structural Transformation* conceptualized the public sphere from the standpoint of a historically specific political project: the democratization of the modern territorial (nation-)state. Far from putting in question that project's Westphalian frame, Habermas envisioned a deliberative model of democracy that was situated squarely within it. In this model, democracy requires the generation, through territorially bounded processes of public communication, conducted in the national language and relayed through the national media, of a body of national public opinion. This opinion should reflect the general interest of the national citizenry concerning the organization of their territorially bounded common life, especially the national economy. The model also requires the mobilization of public opinion as a political force. Effectively empowering the national citizenry, publicity should influence lawmakers and hold state officials accountable. Serving thus to 'rationalize' national political domination, it should ensure that the actions and policies of the Westphalian state reflect the discursively formed political will of the national citizenry. In *Structural Transformation*, therefore, the public sphere is a key institutional component of (national) Westphalian democracy.

Empirically, then, *Structural Transformation* highlighted historical processes, however incomplete, of the democratization of the Westphalian nation-state. Normatively, it articulated a model of deliberative democracy for a territorially bounded polity. Accordingly, the public sphere served as a benchmark for identifying, and critiquing, the democratic deficits of actually existing Westphalian states. Thus, Habermas's early theory enabled us to ask: Are all citizens really full members of the national political public? Can all participate on equal terms? In other words, is what passes as national public opinion genuinely *legitimate*? Moreover, does that opinion attain sufficient political force to rein in private powers and to subject the actions of state officials to citizen control? Does the communicative power generated in Westphalian civil society effectively translate into legislative and administrative power in the Westphalian state? In other words, is national public opinion politically *efficacious*? By inviting us to explore such questions, *Structural Transformation* constituted a contribution to the critique of actually existing democracy in the modern Westphalian state.

Some readers found the critique insufficiently radical. In the discussion that followed the work's belated translation into English, the objections tended to divide into two distinct streams. One stream interrogated the *legitimacy* of public opinion along lines beyond those pursued by Habermas. Focused on relations within civil society, exponents of what I shall call 'the legitimacy critique' contended that *Structural Transformation* obscured the existence of systemic obstacles that deprive some who are nominally members of the public of the capacity to participate on a par with others, as full partners in public debate. Highlighting class inequalities and status hierarchies in civil society, these critics analysed their effects on those whom the Westphalian frame included in principle, but excluded or marginalized in practice: propertyless workers, women, the poor; ethno-racial, religious, and national minorities.[10] Thus, this critique questioned the legitimacy of what passes for public opinion in democratic theory and in social reality.

A second stream of criticism radicalized Habermas's problematization of the *efficacy* of public opinion. Focused on relations between civil society and the state, proponents of 'the efficacy critique' maintained that *Structural Transformation* failed to register the full range of systemic obstacles that deprive discursively generated public opinion of political muscle. Not convinced that these had been adequately captured by Habermas's account of the 'refeudalization' of the public sphere, these critics sought to theorize the structural forces that block the flow of communicative power from civil society to the state. Highlighting the respective roles of private economic power and entrenched bureaucratic interests, their critique served to deepen doubt about the efficacy of public opinion as a political force in capitalist societies.[11]

Notwithstanding the difference in focus, the two streams of criticism shared a deeper assumption. Like *Structural Transformation*, both the legitimacy critics and the efficacy critics took for granted the Westphalian framing of political space. To be sure, some proponents of the legitimacy critique exposed the national subtext of publicity that had largely gone without saying in Habermas's account. Analysing its exclusionary effects on national minorities, multiculturalist critics sought to purge the public sphere of majority national privilege in hopes of reducing disparities of participation in public debate. The point, however, was not to question the territorial basis of the public sphere. Far from casting doubt on the Westphalian frame, the critics sought to enhance the legitimacy of public opinion within it. An analogous objective informed the efficacy critique. Taking for granted that public opinion was addressed to a territorial state, proponents of this critique hoped to subject the latter more firmly to the discursively formed will of its *demos*. Like Habermas, then, if arguably more radically, both sets of critics placed their reflections on the public sphere within the Westphalian frame.

My own earlier effort to 'rethink the public sphere' was no exception. In an article originally published in 1990 (reprinted as Fraser 1992a), I directed criticisms of both types against what I called, following Habermas, 'the liberal model of the bourgeois public sphere'. In its legitimacy aspect, my critique focused on the effects on public opinion of inequality within civil society. Rebutting the liberal view that it was possible for interlocutors in a public sphere to bracket status and class differentials and to deliberate 'as if' they were peers, I argued that social equality is a necessary condition for political democracy. Under real-world conditions of massive *in*equality, I reckoned, the only way to reduce disparities in political voice was through social movement contestation that challenged some basic features of bourgeois publicity. Complicating the standard liberal picture of a single comprehensive public sphere, I claimed that the proliferation of subaltern counterpublics could enhance the participation of subordinate strata in stratified societies. Exposing, too, the bourgeois masculinist bias in standard liberal views of what counts as a public concern, I endorsed efforts by movements such as feminism to redraw the boundaries between public and private. Yet this critique presupposed the national-territorial understanding of publicity. Far from challenging the Westphalian frame, it aimed to enhance the legitimacy of public opinion within it (Fraser 1992a: especially 117–29; see also Fraser 1992b).

My 1990 article just discussed also propounded an efficacy critique, which interrogated the capacity of public opinion to achieve political force. Identifying forces that block the translation of communicative power into administrative power, I questioned the standard liberal view that a functioning public sphere always requires a sharp separation between civil society and the state. Distinguishing the 'weak publics' of civil society, which generate public opinion but not binding laws, from the 'strong publics' within the state, whose deliberations issue in sovereign decisions, I sought to envision institutional arrangements that could enhance the latter's accountability to the former. Aiming, too, to open space for imagining radical-democratic alternatives, I questioned the apparent foreclosure by Habermas of hybrid forms, such as 'quasi-strong' decision-making publics in civil society. Yet here, too, I neglected to challenge the Westphalian frame. The thrust of my argument was, on the contrary, to enhance the efficacy of public opinion vis-à-vis the Westphalian state (see Fraser 1992a: especially 129–32).

Both the legitimacy critique and the efficacy critique still seem right to me as far as they went. But I now believe that neither went far enough. Neither critique interrogated, let alone modified, the social-theoretical underpinnings of *Structural Transformation*, which situated the public sphere in a Westphalian frame. Still oriented to the prospects for deliberative democracy in a bounded political community, both critiques continued to identify the public with the citizenry of a territorial state. Neither abandoned the assumption of a national economy, whose proper steering by the democratic state remained a principal *topos* of public sphere debate, which was itself still envisioned as being conducted in the national language through the national media. Thus, neither the legitimacy critique nor the efficacy critique challenged the Westphalian frame. Animated by the same political project as *Structural Transformation*, both sought to further deliberative democracy in the modern territorial state.

The same is true for Habermas's subsequent discussion of publicity in *Between Facts and Norms* (1996). Among other things, that work revisited the public sphere and incorporated elements of the two critiques. Stressing the 'co-implication of private and public autonomy', Habermas (1996: 420–3) valorized the role of emancipatory social movements, such as second-wave feminism, in promoting democracy by pursuing equality, and vice versa. By thus acknowledging the mutual dependence of social position and political voice, he grappled here with previously neglected aspects of the legitimacy deficits of public opinion in democratic states. In addition, *Between Facts and Norms* was centrally concerned with the problem of efficacy. Theorizing law as the proper vehicle for translating communicative into administrative power, the work distinguished an 'official', democratic circulation of power, in which weak publics influence strong publics, which in turn control administrative state apparatuses, from an 'unofficial', undemocratic one, in which private social powers and entrenched bureaucratic interests control law-makers and manipulate public opinion. Acknowledging that the unofficial circulation usually prevails, Habermas (1996: 360–3) here provided a fuller account of the efficacy deficits of public opinion in democratic states.

One may question, to be sure, whether Habermas fully succeeded in addressing his critics' concerns on either point.[12] But even if we grant him the benefit of that doubt, the fact remains that *Between Facts and Norms* continued to assume the Westphalian frame. Its many departures from *Structural Transformation* notwithstanding, the later work still conceived the addressee of public opinion as a sovereign territorial state, which could steer a national economy in the general interest of the national citizenry; and it still conceived the formation of public opinion as a process conducted in the national media via a national communications infrastructure. Granted, Habermas (1996: 465–6, 500) did advocate a postnationalist form of social integration, namely 'constitutional patriotism', with the aim of emancipating the democratic state from its nationalist integument. But in this he effectively endorsed a more purely Westphalian, because more exclusively territorial, conception of publicity.

In general, then, the publicity debate in critical theory contains a major blind spot. From *Structural Transformation* through *Between Facts and Norms*, virtually all the participants, including me, correlated public spheres with territorial states. Despite their other important disagreements, all assumed the Westphalian framing of political space – at precisely the moment when epochal historical developments seemed to be calling that frame into question.

The Postnational Constellation: Problematizing the Westphalian Frame

Today, the Westphalian blindspot of public-sphere theory is hard to miss. Whether the issue is global warming or immigration, women's rights or the terms of trade, unemployment or 'the war on terror', current mobilizations of public opinion seldom stop at the borders of territorial states. In many cases, the interlocutors do not constitute a *demos* or political citizenry. Often, too, their communications are neither addressed to a Westphalian state nor relayed through national media. Frequently, moreover, the problems debated are inherently trans-territorial and can neither be located within Westphalian space nor be resolved by a Westphalian state. In such cases, current formations of public opinion scarcely respect the parameters of the Westphalian frame. Thus, assumptions that previously went without saying in public-sphere theory now cry out for critique and revision.

No wonder, then, that expressions like 'transnational public spheres', 'diasporic public spheres', and 'the global public sphere' figure so prominently in current discussions. Views about these phenomena divide into two camps. One camp treats transnational publicity as a new development, associated with late twentieth-century globalization. Claiming that the modern interstate system previously channelled most political debate into state-centred discursive arenas, this camp maintains that the Westphalian frame was appropriate for theorizing public spheres until very recently.[13] The second camp insists, in contrast, that publicity has been transnational at least since the origins of the interstate system in the seventeenth century. Citing Enlightenment visions of the international 'republic of letters' and cross-national movements such as abolitionism and socialism, not to mention world religions and modern imperialism, this camp contends that the Westphalian frame has always been ideological, obscuring the inherently unbounded character of public spheres (Boli and Thomas 1999; Keck and Sikkink 1998). Undoubtedly, both interpretations have some merit.

Whereas the first accurately captures the hegemonic division of political space, the second rightly reminds us that metropolitan democracy arose in tandem with colonial subjection, which galvanized transnational flows of public opinion. For present purposes, therefore, I propose to split the difference between them. Granting that transnational publicity has a long history, I shall assume that its present configuration is nevertheless new, reflecting yet another 'structural transformation of the public sphere'. On this point, all parties can surely agree: the current constitution of public opinion bursts open the Westphalian frame.

Yet the full implications remain to be drawn. Focusing largely on cultural aspects of transnational flows, such as 'hybridization' and 'glocalization', many students of transnational publicity neglect to pose the questions of greatest importance for a *critical* theory: If public opinion now overflows the Westphalian frame, what becomes of its *critical* function of checking domination and democratizing governance? More specifically, can we still meaningfully interrogate the *legitimacy* of public opinion when the interlocutors do not constitute a *demos* or political citizenry? And what could legitimacy mean in such a context? Likewise, can we still meaningfully interrogate the *efficacy* of public opinion when it is not addressed to a sovereign state that is capable in principle of regulating its territory and solving its citizens' problems in the public interest? And what could efficacy mean in this situation? Absent satisfactory answers to these questions, we lack a usable *critical* theory of the public sphere.[14]

To clarify the stakes, I propose to revisit the six constitutive presuppositions of public-sphere theory. I shall consider, in the case of each presupposition, how matters stand empirically and what follows for the public sphere's status as a *critical* category.

1 Consider, first, the assumption that the addressee of public opinion is a modern Westphalian state, with exclusive, undivided sovereignty over a bounded territory. Empiri-

cally, this view of sovereignty is highly questionable – and not just for poor and weak states. Today, even powerful states share responsibility for many key governance functions with international institutions, intergovernmental networks, and nongovernmental organizations. This is the case not only for relatively new functions, such as environmental regulation, but also for classical ones, such as defence, policing, and the administration of civil and criminal law – witness the International Atomic Energy Agency, the International Criminal Court, and the World Intellectual Property Organization.[15] Certainly, these institutions are dominated by hegemonic states, as was the interstate system before them. But the mode in which hegemony is exercised today is evidently new. Far from invoking the Westphalian model of exclusive, undivided state sovereignty, hegemony increasingly operates through a *post-Westphalian model of disaggregated sovereignty*.[16] Empirically, therefore, the first presupposition of public-sphere theory does not stand up.

But what follows for public-sphere theory? The effect, I submit, is not simply to falsify the theory's underpinnings, but also to jeopardize the *critical* function of public opinion. If states do not fully control their own territories, if they lack the sole and undivided capacity to wage war, secure order, and administer law, then how can their citizenries' public opinion be politically effective? Even granting, for the sake of argument, that national publicity is fairly generated and satisfies criteria of legitimacy; even granting, too, that it influences the will of parliament and the state administration; how, under conditions of disaggregated sovereignty, can it be *implemented*? How, in sum, can public opinion be *efficacious* as a critical force in a post-Westphalian world?

2 Consider, next, the assumption that a public coincides with a national citizenry, resident on a national territory, which formulates its common interest as the general will of a bounded political community. This assumption, too, is counterfactual. For one thing, the equation of citizenship, nationality, and territorial residence is belied by such

phenomena as migrations, diasporas, dual- and triple-citizenship arrangements, indigenous community member-ship, and patterns of multiple residency. Every state now has non-citizens on its territory; most are multicultural and/or multinational; and every nationality is territorially dispersed.[17] Equally confounding, however, is the fact that public spheres today are not coextensive with political mem-bership. Often the interlocutors are neither co-nationals nor fellow citizens. The opinion they generate, therefore, repre-sents neither the common interest nor the general will of any *demos*. Far from institutionalizing debate among citi-zens who share a common status as political equals, post-Westphalian publicity appears in the eyes of many observers to empower transnational elites, who possess the material and symbolic prerequisites for global networking (Calhoun 2002).

Here, too, the difficulty is not just empirical but also con-ceptual and political. If the interlocutors do not constitute a *demos*, how can their collective opinion be translated into binding laws and administrative policies? If, moreover, they are not fellow citizens, putatively equal in participation rights, status, and voice, then how can the opinion they generate be considered legitimate? How, in sum, can the *critical* criteria of *efficacy* and *legitimacy* be meaningfully applied to transnational public opinion in a post-Westphalian world?

3 Consider, now, the assumption that a principal *topos* of public-sphere discussion is the proper regulation by a territorial state of a national economy. That assumption, too, is belied by present conditions. We need only mention outsourcing, transnational corporations, and offshore busi-ness registry to appreciate that territorially based national production is now largely notional. Thanks, moreover, to the dismantling of the Bretton Woods capital controls and the emergence of 24/7 global electronic financial markets, state control over national currency is presently quite limited. Finally, as those who protest policies of the World Trade

Organization, the International Monetary Fund, the North American Free Trade Agreement, and the World Bank have insisted, the ground rules governing trade, production, and finance are set transnationally, by agencies more accountable to global capital than to any public.[18] In these conditions, the presupposition of a national economy is counterfactual.

As before, moreover, the effect is to imperil the critical function of public spheres. If states cannot in principle steer economies in line with the articulated general interest of their populations, how can national public opinion be an effective force? Then, too, if economic governance is in the hands of agencies that are not locatable in Westphalian space, how can it be made accountable to public opinion? Moreover, if those agencies are invalidating national labour and environmental laws in the name of free trade, if they are prohibiting domestic social spending in the name of structural adjustment, if they are institutionalizing neoliberal governance rules that would once and for all remove major matters of public concern from any possibility of political regulation, if in sum they are systematically reversing the democratic project, using markets to tame politics instead of politics to tame markets, then how can citizen public opinion have any impact? Lastly, if the world capitalist system operates to the massive detriment of the global poor, how can what passes for transnational public opinion be remotely legitimate, when those affected by current policies cannot possibly debate their merits as peers? In general, then, how can public opinion concerning the economy be either *legitimate* or *efficacious* in a post-Westphalian world?

4 Consider, as well, the assumption that public opinion is conveyed through a national communications infrastructure, centred on print and broadcasting. This assumption implies that communicative processes, however decentred, are sufficiently coherent and politically focused to coalesce in 'public opinion'. But it, too, is rendered counterfactual by current conditions. Recall the profusion of niche media, some subnational, some transnational, which do not in any

case function as national media, focused on subjecting the exercise of state power to the test of publicity. Granted, one can also note the parallel emergence of global media, but these market-driven, corporately owned outlets are scarcely focused on checking transnational power. In addition, many countries have privatized government-operated media, with decidedly mixed results: on the one hand, the prospect of a more independent press and TV and more inclusive populist programming; on the other hand, the further spread of market logic, advertisers' power, and dubious amalgams like talk radio and 'infotainment'. Finally, we should mention instantaneous electronic, broadband, and satellite communi-cations technologies, which permit direct transnational communication, bypassing state controls. Together, all these developments signal the denationalization of communicative infrastructure.[19]

The effects here too pose threats to the critical functioning of public spheres. Granted, we see some new opportunities for critical public opinion formation. But these go along with the disaggregation and complexification of communicative flows. Given a field divided between corporate global media, restricted niche media, and decentred internet networks, how could critical public opinion possibly be generated on a large scale and mobilized as a political force? Given, too, the absence of even the sort of formal equality associated with common citizenship, how could those who comprise trans-national media audiences deliberate together as peers? How, once again, can public opinion be normatively *legitimate* or politically *efficacious* under current conditions?

5 Consider, too, the presupposition of a single national language, which was supposed to constitute the linguistic medium of public-sphere communication. As a result of the population mixing already noted, national languages do not map onto states. The problem is not simply that official state languages were consolidated at the expense of local and regional dialects, although they were. It is also that existing states are *de facto* multilingual, while language groups are

territorially dispersed, and many more speakers are multi-lingual. Meanwhile, English has become the *lingua franca* of global business, mass entertainment, and academia. Yet language remains a political fault-line, threatening to explode countries like Belgium, if no longer Canada, while compli-cating efforts to democratize countries like South Africa and to erect transnational formations like the European Union.[20] These developments, too, pose threats to the critical func-tion of public opinion. Insofar as public spheres are mono-lingual, how can they constitute an inclusive communications community of all those affected? Conversely, insofar as public spheres correspond to linguistic communities that straddle political boundaries and do not correspond to any citizenry, how can they mobilize public opinion as a political force? Likewise, insofar as new transnational political com-munities, such as the EU, are transnational and multi-linguistic, how can they constitute public spheres that can encompass the entire *demos*? Finally, insofar as transna-tional publics conduct their communications in English, which favours global elites and Anglophone postcolonials at the expense of others, how can the opinion they generate be viewed as legitimate? For all these reasons, and in all these ways, language issues compromise both the *legitimacy* and *efficacy* of public opinion in a post-Westphalian world.

6 Consider, finally, the assumption that a public sphere rests on a national vernacular literature, which supplies the shared social imaginary needed to underpin solidarity. This assumption, too, is today counterfactual. Consider the increased salience of cultural hybridity and hybridization, including the rise of 'world literature'. Consider also the rise of global mass entertainment, whether straightforwardly American or merely stylistically informed by American entertainment. Consider, finally, the spectacular rise of visual culture, or, better, of the enhanced salience of the visual within culture, and the relative decline of print and the liter-ary.[21] In all these cases, it is difficult to recognize the sort of (national) literary cultural formation seen by Habermas (and

by Benedict Anderson [1991]) as underpinning the subjective stance of public-sphere interlocutors. On the contrary, insofar as public spheres require the cultural support of shared social imaginaries, rooted in national literary cultures, it is hard to see them functioning effectively today.

In general, then, public spheres are increasingly transnational or postnational with respect to each of the constitutive elements of public opinion.[22] The 'who' of communication, previously theorized as a Westphalian-national citizenry, is often now a collection of dispersed interlocutors, who do not constitute a *demos*. The 'what' of communication, previously theorized as a Westphalian-national interest rooted in a Westphalian-national economy, now stretches across vast reaches of the globe, in a transnational community of risk, which is not, however, reflected in concomitantly expansive solidarities and identities. The 'where' of communication, once theorized as the Westphalian-national territory, is now deterritorialized cyberspace. The 'how' of communication, once theorized as Westphalian-national print media, now encompasses a vast translinguistic nexus of disjoint and overlapping visual cultures. Finally, the 'to whom' or addressee of communication, once theorized as a sovereign territorial state, which should be made answerable to public opinion, is now an amorphous mix of public and private transnational powers that is neither easily identifiable nor easily rendered accountable.

Rethinking the Public Sphere – Yet Again

These developments raise the question of whether and how public spheres today could conceivably perform the democratic political functions with which they have been associated historically. Could public spheres today conceivably generate *legitimate* public opinion, in the strong sense of considered understandings of the general interest, filtered through fair and inclusive argumentation, open to everyone potentially affected? And if so, how? Likewise, could public spheres today conceivably render public opinion sufficiently *efficacious* to constrain the various powers that determine the conditions of the interlocutors' lives? And if so, how? What sorts of changes (institutional, economic, cultural, and communicative) would be required even to imagine a genuinely *critical* and democratizing role for transnational public spheres under current conditions? Where are the sovereign powers that public opinion today should constrain? Which publics are relevant to which powers? Who are the relevant members of a given public? In what language(s) and through what media should they communicate? And via what communicative infrastructure?

These questions well exceed the scope of the present inquiry. And I shall not pretend to try to answer them here. I want to conclude, rather, by suggesting a conceptual strategy that can clarify the issues and point the way to possible resolutions.

My proposal centres on the two features that together constituted the *critical* force of the concept of the public sphere in the Westphalian era: namely, the *normative legitimacy* and *political efficacy* of public opinion. As I see it, these ideas are intrinsic, indispensable elements of *any* conception of publicity that purports to be critical, regardless of the socio-historical conditions in which it obtains. The present constellation is no exception. Unless we can envision conditions under which current flows of transnational publicity could conceivably become legitimate and efficacious, the concept loses its critical edge and its political point. Thus, the only way to salvage the critical function of publicity today is to rethink legitimacy and efficacy. The task is to detach those two ideas from the Westphalian premises that previously underpinned them and to reconstruct them for a post-Westphalian world.

Consider, first, the question of *legitimacy*. In public-sphere theory, as we saw, public opinion is considered legitimate if and only if all who are potentially affected are able to participate as peers in deliberations concerning the organization of their common affairs. In effect, then, the theory holds that

the legitimacy of public opinion is a function of two analytically distinct characteristics of the communicative process,
namely, the extent of its *inclusiveness* and the degree to
which it realizes *participatory parity*. In the first case, which
I shall call the inclusiveness condition, discussion must in
principle be open to all with a stake in the outcome. In the
second, which I shall call the parity condition, all interlocutors must, in principle, enjoy roughly equal chances to state
their views, place issues on the agenda, question the tacit
and explicit assumptions of others, switch levels as needed,
and generally receive a fair hearing. Whereas the inclusiveness condition concerns the question of *who* is authorized to
participate in public discussions, the parity condition concerns the question of *how*, in the sense of on what terms, the
interlocutors engage one another.[23]
In the past, however, these two legitimacy conditions of
public opinion were not always clearly distinguished. Seen
from the perspective of the Westphalian frame, both the
inclusiveness condition and the parity condition were yoked
together under the ideal of *shared citizenship in a bounded
community*. As we saw, public-sphere theorists implicitly
assumed that citizenship set the legitimate bounds of inclusion, effectively equating those affected with the members
of an established polity. Tacitly, too, theorists appealed to
citizenship in order to give flesh to the idea of parity of participation in public deliberations, effectively associating communicative parity with the shared status of political equality
in a territorial state. Thus, citizenship supplied the model for
both the 'who' and the 'how' of legitimate public opinion in
the Westphalian frame.
The effect, however, was to truncate discussions of legitimacy. Although it went unnoticed at the time, the Westphalian frame encouraged debate about the parity condition,
while deflecting attention away from the inclusiveness condition. Taking for granted the modern territorial state as the
appropriate unit, and its citizens as the pertinent subjects,
that frame foregrounded the question of *how* precisely those
citizens should relate to one another in the public sphere.

The argument focused, in other words, on what should count as a relation of participatory parity among the members of a bounded political community. Engrossed in disputing the 'how' of legitimacy, the contestants apparently felt no necessity to dispute the 'who'. With the Westphalian frame securely in place, it went without saying that the 'who' was the national citizenry.

Today, however, the question of the 'who' can no longer be swept under the carpet. Under current conditions of transnationality, the inclusiveness condition of legitimacy cries out for explicit interrogation. We must ask: If political citizenship no longer suffices to demarcate the members of the public, then how should the inclusiveness requirement be understood? By what alternative criterion should we determine who counts as a bonafide interlocutor in a post-Westphalian public sphere?

Public-sphere theory already offers a clue. In its classical Habermasian form, the theory associates the idea of inclusiveness with the 'all-affected principle'. Applying that principle to publicity, it holds that all potentially affected by political decisions should have the chance to participate on terms of parity in the informal processes of opinion formation to which the decision-makers should be accountable. Everything depends, accordingly, on how one interprets the all-affected principle. Previously, public-sphere theorists assumed, in keeping with the Westphalian frame, that what most affected people's life conditions was the constitutional order of the territorial state of which they were citizens. As a result, it seemed that in correlating publics with political citizenship, one simultaneously captured the force of the all-affected principle. In fact, this was never truly so, as the long history of colonialism and neocolonialism attests. From the perspective of the metropole, however, the conflation of membership with affectedness appeared to have an emancipatory thrust, as it served to justify the progressive incorporation, as active citizens, of the subordinate classes and status groups who were resident on the territory but excluded from full political participation.

Today, however, the idea that citizenship can serve as a proxy for affectedness is no longer plausible. Under current conditions, one's conditions of living do not depend wholly on the internal constitution of the political community of which one is a citizen. Although the latter remains undeniably relevant, its effects are mediated by other structures, both extra- and non-territorial, whose impact is at least as significant.[24] In general, globalization is driving a widening wedge between affectedness and political membership. As those two notions increasingly diverge, the effect is to reveal the former as an inadequate surrogate for the latter. And so the question arises: Why not apply the all-affected principle directly to the framing of publicity, without going through the detour of citizenship?

Here, I submit, is a promising path for reconstructing a critical conception of inclusive public opinion in a post-Westphalian world.[25] Although I cannot explore this path fully here, let me note the essential point: the all-affected principle holds that what turns a collection of people into fellow members of a public is not shared citizenship, but their co-imbrication in a common set of structures and/or institutions that affect their lives. For any given problem, accordingly, the relevant public should match the reach of those life-conditioning structures whose effects are at issue (see Fraser 2008: ch. 2). Where such structures transgress the borders of states, the corresponding public spheres must be transnational. Failing that, the opinion that they generate cannot be considered legitimate.

With respect to the legitimacy of public opinion, then, the challenge is clear. In order for public-sphere theory to retain its critical orientation in a post-Westphalian world, it must reinterpret the meaning of the inclusiveness requirement. Renouncing the automatic identification of the latter with political citizenship, it must redraw publicity's boundaries by applying the all-affected principle directly to the question at hand. In this way, the question of the 'who' emerges from under its Westphalian veil. Along with the question of the 'how', which remains as pressing as ever, it, too, becomes an explicit focus of concern in the present constellation. In fact, the two questions, that of inclusiveness and that of parity, now go hand in hand. Henceforth, public opinion is legitimate if and only if it results from a communicative process in which all potentially affected can participate as peers, *regardless of political citizenship*. Demanding as it is, this new, post-Westphalian understanding of legitimacy constitutes a genuinely critical standard for evaluating existing forms of publicity in the present era.

Let me turn, now, to the second essential feature of a critical conception of publicity, namely, the political *efficacy* of public opinion. In public-sphere theory, as we saw, public opinion is considered efficacious if and only if it is mobilized as a political force to hold public power accountable, ensuring that the latter's exercise reflects the considered will of civil society. In effect, therefore, the theory treats publicity's efficacy as a function of two distinct elements, which I shall call the *translation* condition and the *capacity* condition. According to the translation condition, the communicative power generated in civil society must be translated first into binding laws and then into administrative power. According to the capacity condition, the public power must be able to implement the discursively formed will to which it is responsible. Whereas the translation condition concerns the flow of communicative power from civil society to an instituted public power, the capacity condition concerns the ability of an administrative power to realize its public's designs, both negatively, by reining in private powers, and positively, by solving its problems and organizing common life in accord with its wishes.

In the past, these two efficacy conditions were understood in the light of the Westphalian frame. From that perspective, both the translation condition and the capacity condition were linked to the idea of the sovereign territorial state. As we saw, public-sphere theorists assumed that the addressee of public opinion was the Westphalian state, which should be constituted democratically, so that communication flows unobstructed from weak publics to strong publics, where it can be translated into binding laws. At the same time, these theorists also assumed that the Westphalian state had the necessary administrative capacity to implement those laws so as to realize its citizens' aims and solve their problems. Thus, the Westphalian state was considered the proper vehicle for fulfilling both the translation and capacity conditions of public-sphere efficacy.

Here, too, however, the result was to truncate discussions of efficacy. Although the Westphalian frame fostered interest in the translation condition, it tended to obscure the capacity condition. Taking for granted that the sovereign territorial state was the proper addressee of public opinion, that frame foregrounded the question of whether the communicative power generated in the national public sphere was sufficiently strong to influence legislation and constrain state administration. The argument focused, accordingly, on what should count as a democratic circulation of power between civil society and the state. What was not much debated, in contrast, was the state's capacity to regulate the private powers that shaped its citizens' lives. That issue went without saying, as public-sphere theorists assumed, for example, that economies were effectively national and could be steered by national states in the interest of national citizens. Engrossed in debating the translation condition, they apparently felt no necessity to dispute the capacity condition. With the Westphalian frame in place, the latter became a non-issue.

Today, however, these assumptions no longer hold. Under current conditions of transnationality, the capacity condition demands interrogation in its own right. We must ask: If the modern territorial state no longer possesses the administrative ability to steer 'its' economy, ensure the integrity of 'its' national environment, and provide for the security and well-being of 'its' citizens, then how should we understand the capacity component of efficacy today? By what means can the requisite administrative capacity be constituted and where precisely should it be lodged? If not to the sovereign territorial state, then to what or whom should public opinion on transnational problems be addressed?

With respect to these questions, existing public-sphere theory affords few clues. But it does suggest that the problem of publicity's efficacy in a post-Westphalian world is doubly complicated. A critical conception can no longer restrict its attention to the direction of communicative flows in established polities, where publicity should constrain an already known and constituted addressee. In addition, it must consider the need to construct new addressees for public opinion, in the sense of new, transnational public powers that possess the administrative capacity to solve transnational problems. The challenge, accordingly, is twofold: on the one hand, to create new, transnational public powers; on the other, to make them accountable to new, transnational public spheres. Both those elements are necessary; neither alone is sufficient. Only if it thematizes both conditions (capacity as well as translation) will public-sphere theory develop a post-Westphalian conception of communicative efficacy that is genuinely critical.

In general, then, the task is clear: if public-sphere theory is to function today as a *critical* theory, it must revise its account of the normative legitimacy and political efficacy of public opinion. No longer content to leave half the picture in the shadows, it must treat each of those notions as comprising two analytically distinct but practically entwined critical requirements. Thus, the legitimacy critique of existing publicity must now interrogate not only the 'how' but also the 'who' of existing publicity. Or, rather, it must interrogate parity and inclusiveness together, by asking: *participatory parity among whom?* Likewise, the efficacy critique must now be expanded to encompass both the translation and capacity conditions of existing publicity. Putting those two requirements together, it must envision new transnational public powers, which can be made accountable to new democratic transnational circuits of public opinion.

Granted, the job is not easy. But only if public-sphere theory rises to the occasion can it serve as a *critical* theory in a post-Westphalian world. For that purpose, it is not enough for cultural studies and media studies scholars to map existing communications flows. Rather, critical social and political theorists will need to rethink the theory's core premises concerning the legitimacy and efficacy of public opinion. Only then will the theory recover its critical edge and its political point. Only then will public-sphere theory keep faith with its original promise to contribute to struggles for emancipation.

Notes

Minor stylistic alterations aside, this chapter reprints the text published as chapter 5 in *Scales of Justice* (2008). Thus, it differs in one substantive respect from the original version published in *Theory, Culture & Society* 24(4) (2007): 7–30. Whereas the 2007 version appealed without qualification to the 'all-affected principle' as the standard for evaluating the inclusiveness of public spheres and the legitimacy of the public opinion generated within them, this one includes a note explaining that I have since abandoned that idea in favour of the 'all-subjected principle'. I explain the reasons for this shift in chapter 4 ('Abnormal Justice') of *Scales of Justice* and in chapter 7 ('Publicity, Subjection, Critique') of the present volume.

1 See, for example, Bowen 2004; Guidry et al. 2000; Mules 1998; Olesen 2005; Stichweh 2003; Tololyan 1996; Volkmer 2003; and Werbner 2004.
2 See, above all, Habermas 1989: especially 51–6, 140, 222ff.; and Habermas 1996: especially 359–79.
3 For an explanation of my use of the term 'Westphalian', see Fraser 2008: 160–1.
4 Habermas 1989: 14–26, 79–88; see also Habermas 1996: 135–8, 141–4, 352, 366–7, 433–6.
5 Habermas 1989: 20–4, 51–7, 62–73, 83–8, 141ff.; see also Habermas 1996: 365–6, 381–7.
6 Habermas 1989: 14–20, especially 17; see also Habermas 1996: 344–51, especially 349–50.
7 Habermas 1989: 58, 60–70; see also Habermas 1996: 373–4, 376–7.
8 Habermas 1989: 24–39, especially 36–7, 55–6, 60–73; see also Habermas 1996: 360–2, 369–70, 375–7.

9 Habermas 1989: 41–3, 48–51; see also Habermas 1996: 373–4. The phrase 'print capitalism' is not Habermas's, but Benedict Anderson's (see Anderson 1991).

10 Black Public Sphere Collective 1995; Brooks-Higginbotham 1993; Eley 1992; Gole 1997; James 1999; Landes 1988; Rendall 1999; Ryan 1990, 1995; Soysal 1997; Warner 2002; Young 1987.

11 An early form of this critique can be found in Luhmann 1970. See also Aronowitz 1993; Garnham 1995; Gerhards and Neidhardt 1990; Warner 1993.

12 According to William E. Scheuerman (1999a), for example, Habermas oscillates inconsistently between two antithetical stances: on the one hand, a 'realistic', resigned, objectively conservative view that accepts the grave legitimacy and efficacy deficits of public opinion in really existing democratic states; on the other, a radical-democratic view that is still committed to overcoming them. I suspect that Scheuerman may well be right. Nevertheless, for purposes of the present argument, I shall stipulate that Habermas convincingly negotiates the tension 'between fact and norm' in the democratic state.

13 Ferguson and Jones 2002; Held 1995; Held et al. 1999; Sassen 1998, 2006.

14 Some scholars do raise these questions. For genuinely critical treatments, see Bohman 1997, 1998; Lara 2003.

15 Held et al. 1999; Rosenau 1997, 1999; Scheuerman 1999b; Schneiderman 2001; Slaughter 2005; Strange 1996; Zacher 1992.

16 Hardt and Negri 2001; Pangalangan 2001; Sassen 1995; Strange 1996.

17 Aleynikoff and Klusmeyer 1995; Benhabib 2002, 2004; Husband 1996; Linklater 1999; Preuss 1999.

18 Cerny 1997; Germain 2004; Held et al. 1999; Helleiner 1994; Perraton et al. 1997; Schulze 2000; Stetting et al. 1999; Stiglitz 2003.

19 Cammaerts and van Audenhove 2005; Dahlgren 2005; Held et al. 1999; McChesney 1999, 2001; Papacharissi 2002; Yudice 2004.

20 Adrey 2005; Alexander 2003; König 1999; Patten 2001; Phillipson 2003; Shabani 2004; Van Parijs 2000; Wilkinson 2004.

21 Appadurai 1996; DeLuca and Peeples 2002; Hannerz 1996; Jameson 1998; Marshall 2004; Yudice 2004.

22 Habermas (2001) has himself remarked many of the developments cited above that problematize the Westphalian presuppositions of public-sphere theory.
23 Certainly, these conditions are highly idealized and never fully
met in practice. But it is precisely their idealized character that
ensured the *critical* force of public-sphere theory. By appealing
to the standard of inclusive communication among peers, the
theory was able to criticize existing, power-skewed processes
of publicity. By exposing unjustified exclusions and disparities,
the theory was able to motivate its addressees to try to overcome them.
24 Pogge 2002, especially the sections on 'The Causal Role of
Global Institutions in the Persistence of Severe Poverty',
112–16, and 'Explanatory Nationalism: The Deep Significance
of National Borders', 139–44.
25 Since writing this chapter, however, I have discovered a more
promising path. For reasons explained in chapter 4 of *Scales
of Justice* (Fraser 2008), I now believe that the all-subjected
principle represents an advance over the approach discussed
here. Thus, I propose in future work to develop a modified
form of the Habermasian discourse principle, centred on the
idea that what turns a collection of people into fellow members
of a public is not shared citizenship, but their joint subjection
to governance structures, which set the ground rules for their
interaction. For any given problem, accordingly, the relevant
public should match the reach of the governance structures
which regulate the interactions at issue.

References

Adrey, J.-B. (2005) 'Minority Language Rights Before and After
the 2004 EU Enlargement: The Copenhagen Criteria in the
Baltic States', *Journal of Multilingual & Multicultural Devel-
opment* 26(5): 453–68.
Alexander, N. (2003) 'Language Policy, Symbolic Power and the
Democratic Responsibility of the Post-Apartheid University',
Pretexts: Literary & Cultural Studies 12(2): 179–90.
Aleynikoff, T.A. and D. Klusmeyer (2001) *Citizenship Today:
Global Perspectives and Practices*. Washington, DC: Carnegie
Endowment for Peace.

Anderson, B. (1991) *Imagined Communities: Reflections on the Origin and Spread of Nationalism*, 2nd edn. London: Verso.

Appadurai, A. (1996) *Modernity at Large: Cultural Dimensions of Globalization*. Minneapolis: University of Minnesota Press.

Aronowitz, S. (1993) 'Is a Democracy Possible? The Decline of the Public in the American Debate', in B. Robbins (ed.), *The Phantom Public Sphere*. Minneapolis: University of Minnesota Press.

Benhabib, S. (2002) 'Transformations of Citizenship: The Case of Contemporary Europe', *Government and Opposition: An International Journal of Comparative Politics* 37(4): 439–65.

Benhabib, S. (2004) *The Rights of Others: Aliens, Residents, and Citizens*. Cambridge: Cambridge University Press.

Black Public Sphere Collective (1995) *The Black Public Sphere*. Chicago: University of Chicago Press.

Bohman, J. (1997) 'The Public Spheres of the World Citizen', in J. Bohman and M. Lutz-Bachmann (eds), *Perpetual Peace: Essays on Kant's Cosmopolitan Ideal*. Cambridge, MA: MIT Press.

Bohman, J. (1998) 'The Globalization of the Public Sphere: Cosmopolitan Publicity and the Problem of Cultural Pluralism', *Philosophy and Social Criticism* 24(2–3): 199–216.

Boli, J. and J. Thomas (1999) *Constructing World Culture: International Nongovernmental Organizations Since 1875*. Stanford: Stanford University Press.

Bowen, J.R. (2004) 'Beyond Migration: Islam as a Transnational Public Space', *Journal of Ethnic & Migration Studies* 30(5): 879–94.

Brooks-Higginbotham, E. (1993) *Righteous Discontent: The Women's Movement in the Black Baptist Church, 1880–1920*. Cambridge, MA: Harvard University Press.

Calhoun, C. (2002) 'Imagining Solidarity: Cosmopolitanism, Constitutional Patriotism, and the Public Sphere', *Public Culture* 14(1): 147–71.

Cammaerts, B. and L. van Audenhove (2005) 'Online Political Debate, Unbounded Citizenship, and the Problematic Nature of a Transnational Public Sphere', *Political Communication* 22(2): 179–96.

Cerny, P. (1997) 'Paradoxes of the Competition State: The Dynamics of Political Globalization', *Government and Opposition* 32(2): 251–74.

Dahlgren, P. (2005) 'The Internet, Public Spheres, and Political Communication: Dispersion and Deliberation', *Political Communication* 22(2): 147–62.

DeLuca, K.M. and J. Peeples (2002) 'From Public Sphere to Public Screen: Democracy, Activism, and the "Violence" of Seattle', *Critical Studies in Media Communication* 19(2): 125–51.

Eley, G. (1992) 'Nations, Publics, and Political Cultures: Placing Habermas in the Nineteenth Century', in C. Calhoun (ed.), *Habermas and the Public Sphere*. Cambridge, MA: MIT Press.

Ferguson, Y.H. and B. Jones (eds) (2002) *Political Space: Frontiers of Change and Governance in a Globalizing World*. Albany: State University of New York Press.

Fraser, N. (1992a) 'Rethinking the Public Sphere: A Contribution to the Critique of Actually Existing Democracy', in C. Calhoun (ed.), *Habermas and the Public Sphere*. Cambridge MA: MIT Press.

Fraser, N. (1992b) 'Sex, Lies, and the Public Sphere: Some Reflections on the Confirmation of Clarence Thomas', *Critical Inquiry* 18, 595–612.

Fraser, N. (2008) *Scales of Justice: Reimagining Political Space in a Globalizing World*. Cambridge: Polity.

Garnham, N. (1995) 'The Media and the Public Sphere', in C. Calhoun (ed.), *Habermas and the Public Sphere*. Cambridge, MA: MIT Press.

Gerhards, J. and F. Neidhardt (1990) *Strukturen und Funktionen Moderner Öffentlichkeit*. Berlin: Fragestellungen und Ansätze.

Germain, R. (2004) 'Globalising Accountability within the International Organisation of Credit: Financial Governance and the Public Sphere', *Global Society: Journal of Interdisciplinary International Relations* 18(3): 217–42.

Gole, N. (1997) 'The Gendered Nature of the Public Sphere', *Public Culture* 10(1): 61–80.

Guidry, J., M.D. Kennedy, and M.N. Zald (eds) (2000) *Globalizations and Social Movements: Culture, Power, and the Transnational Public Sphere*. Ann Arbor: University of Michigan Press.

Habermas, J. (1989) *The Structural Transformation of the Public Sphere: An Inquiry into a Category of Bourgeois Society*, trans. T. Burger with F. Lawrence. Cambridge: Polity.

Habermas, J. (1996) *Between Facts and Norms: Contributions to a Discourse Theory of Law and Democracy*, trans. W. Rehg. Cambridge: Polity.

Habermas, J. (1998) 'The European Nation-State: On the Past and Future of Sovereignty and Citizenship', *Public Culture* 10(2): 397–416.

Habermas, J. (2001) 'The Postnational Constellation and the Future of Democracy', in *The Postnational Constellation*, trans. and ed. M. Pensky. Cambridge MA: MIT Press.

Hannerz, U. (1996) *Transnational Connections: Culture, People, Places*. New York: Routledge.

Hardt, M. and A. Negri (2001) *Empire*. Cambridge MA: Harvard University Press.

Held, D. (1995) *Democracy and the Global Order: From the Modern State to Cosmopolitical Governance*. Cambridge: Polity Press.

Held, D., A. McGrew, D. Goldblatt, and J. Perraton (1999) *Global Transformations: Politics, Economics and Culture*. Cambridge: Polity.

Helleiner, E. (1994) 'From Bretton Woods to Global Finance: A World Turned Upside Down', in R. Stubbs and G.R.D. Underhill (eds), *Political Economy and the Changing Global Order*. New York: St Martin's Press.

Husband, C. (1996) 'The Right to be Understood: Conceiving the Multi-Ethnic Public Sphere', *Innovation: The European Journal of Social Sciences* 9(2): 205–15.

James, M.R. (1999) 'Tribal Sovereignty and the Intercultural Public Sphere', *Philosophy & Social Criticism* 25(5): 57–86.

Jameson, F. (1998) *The Cultural Turn*. London: Verso.

Keck, M.E. and K. Sikkink (1998) *Activists beyond Borders: Advocacy Networks in International Politics*. Ithaca, NY: Cornell University Press.

König, M. (1999) 'Cultural Diversity and Language Policy', *International Social Science Journal* 51(161): 401–8.

Landes, J. (1988) *Women and the Public Sphere in the Age of the French Revolution*. Ithaca NY: Cornell University Press.

Lara, M.P. (2003) 'Globalizing Women's Rights: Building a Public Sphere', in R.N. Fiore and H.L. Nelson (eds), *Recognition, Responsibility, and Rights: Feminist Ethics and Social Theory. Feminist Reconstructions*. Totowa, NJ: Rowman & Littlefield.

Linklater, A. (1999) 'Citizenship and Sovereignty in the Post-Westphalian European State', in D. Archibugi and D. Held (eds), *Re-imagining Political Community: Studies in Cosmo-politan Democracy*. Stanford: Stanford University Press.

Luhmann, N. (1970) 'Öffentliche Meinung', *Politische Viertel-jahresschrift* 11, 2–28.

McChesney, R.W. (1999) *Rich Media, Poor Democracy: Com-munications Politics in Dubious Times*. Urbana: University of Illinois Press.

McChesney, R.W. (2001) 'Global Media, Neoliberalism, and Imperialism', *Monthly Review* 50(10): 1–19.

Marshall, P.D. (2004) *New Media Cultures*. New York: Oxford University Press.

Mules, W. (1998) 'Media Publics and the Transnational Public Sphere', *Critical Arts Journal* 12(1/2): 24–44.

Olesen, T. (2005) 'Transnational Publics: New Spaces of Social Movement Activism and the Problem of Global Long-Sightedness', *Current Sociology* 53(3): 419–40.

Pangalangan, R.C. (2001) 'Territorial Sovereignty: Command, Title, and Expanding the Claims of the Commons', in D. Miller and S.H. Hashmi (eds), *Boundaries and Justice: Diverse Ethical Perspectives*. Princeton: Princeton University Press.

Papacharissi, Z. (2002) 'The Virtual Sphere: The Internet as a Public Sphere', *New Media & Society* 4(1): 9–36.

Patten, A. (2001) 'Political Theory and Language Policy', *Political Theory* 29(5): 691–715.

Perraton, J., D. Goldblatt, D. Held, and A. McGrew (1997) 'The Globalisation of Economic Activity', *New Political Economy* 2(2): 257–77.

Phillipson, R. (2003) *English-Only Europe? Challenging Lan-guage Policy*. New York: Routledge.

Pogge, T.W. (2002) *World and Poverty and Human Rights: Cosmopolitan Responsibilities and Reforms*. Cambridge: Polity.

Preuss, U. (1999) 'Citizenship in the European Union: A Paradigm for Transnational Democracy?', in D. Archibugi and D. Held (eds), *Re-imagining Political Community: Studies in Cosmo-politan Democracy*. Stanford: Stanford University Press.

Rendall, J. (1999) 'Women and the Public Sphere', *Gender & History* 11(3): 475–89.

Rosenau, J.N. (1997) *Along the Domestic–Foreign Frontier: Exploring Governance in a Turbulent World*. Cambridge: Cambridge University Press.

Rosenau, J.N. (1999) 'Governance and Democracy in a Globalizing World', in D. Archibugi and D. Held (eds), *Re-imagining Political Community: Studies in Cosmopolitan Democracy*. Stanford: Stanford University Press.

Ryan, M.P. (1990) *Women in Public: Between Banners and Ballots, 1825–1880*. Baltimore: Johns Hopkins University Press.

Ryan, M.P. (1995) 'Gender and Public Access: Women's Politics in Nineteenth-Century America', in C. Calhoun (ed.), *Habermas and the Public Sphere*. Cambridge, MA: MIT Press.

Sassen, S. (1995) *Losing Control? Sovereignty in an Age of Globalization*. New York: Columbia University Press.

Sassen, S. (1998) *Globalization and Its Discontents*. New York: Free Press.

Sassen, S. (2006) *Territory, Authority, Rights: From Medieval to Global Assemblages*. Princeton: Princeton University Press.

Scheuerman, W.E. (1999a) 'Between Radicalism and Resignation: Democratic Theory in Habermas' *Between Facts and Norms*', in P. Dews (ed.), *Habermas: A Critical Companion*. Oxford: Blackwell.

Scheuerman, W.E. (1999b) 'Economic Globalization and the Rule of Law', *Constellations* 6(1): 3–25.

Schneiderman, D. (2001) 'Investment Rules and the Rule of Law', *Constellations* 8(4): 521–37.

Schulze, G.G. (2000) *The Political Economy of Capital Controls*. Cambridge: Cambridge University Press.

Shabani, O.A.P. (2004) 'Language Policy and Diverse Societies: Constitutional Patriotism and Minority Language Rights', *Constellations* 11(2): 193–216.

Slaughter A.-M. (2005) *A New World Order*. Princeton: Princeton University Press.

Soysal, Y.N. (1997) 'Changing Parameters of Citizenship and Claims-Making: Organized Islam in European Public Spheres', *Theory and Society* 26, 509–27.

Stetting, L., K.E. Svendsen, and E. Yndgaard (eds) (1999) *Global Change and Transformation: Economic Essays in Honor of Karsten Laursen*. Copenhagen: Handelshojskolens Forlag.

Stichweh, R. (2003) 'The Genesis of a Global Public Sphere', *Development* 46(1): 26–9.

Stiglitz, J.E. (2003) *Globalization and Its Discontents*. New York: Norton.

Strange, S. (1996) *The Retreat of the State: The Diffusion of Power in the World Economy*. Cambridge: Cambridge University Press.

Tololyan, K. (1996) 'Rethinking Diaspora(s): Stateless Power in the Transnational Moment', *Diaspora* 5(1): 3–36.

Van Parijs, P. (2000) 'The Ground Floor of the World: On the Socio-economic Consequences of Linguistic Globalization', *International Political Science Review* 21(2): 217–33.

Volkmer, I. (2003) 'The Global Network Society and the Global Public Sphere', *Development* 46(1): 9–16.

Warner, M. (1993) 'The Mass Public and the Mass Subject', in B. Robbins (ed.), *The Phantom Public Sphere*. Minneapolis: University of Minnesota Press.

Warner, M. (2002) *Publics and Counterpublics*. New York: Zone Books.

Werbner, P. (2004) 'Theorising Complex Diasporas: Purity and Hybridity in the South Asian Public Sphere in Britain', *Journal of Ethnic & Migration Studies* 30(5): 895–911.

Wilkinson, K.T. (2004) 'Language Difference and Communication Policy in the Information Age', *Information Society* 20(3): 217–29.

Young, I.M. (1987) 'Impartiality and the Civic Public: Some Implications of Feminist Critiques of Moral and Political Theory', in S. Benhabib and D. Cornell (eds), *Feminism as Critique*. Minneapolis: University of Minnesota Press.

Yudice, G. (2004) *The Expediency of Culture: Uses of Culture in the Global Era*. Durham, NC: Duke University Press.

Zacher, M.W. (1992) 'The Decaying Pillars of the Westphalian Temple', in J.N. Rosenau and E.-O. Czempiel (eds), *Governance without Government*. Cambridge: Cambridge University Press.

2

What and Where is the Transnationalized Public Sphere?

Nick Couldry

Public-sphere theory encourages us, rightly, to focus on the *tension-ridden* space where discursive practices and normative requirements meet. How we think of that space has been transformed since Habermas's early formulations: no longer face-to-face but inherently mediated,[1] no longer singular but inevitably plural,[2] no longer single-level but multi-level and networked.[3] It is too easy, however, to assume that, merely by becoming more complex, public-sphere theory has become more adequate to the actual space of mediated politics (Curran 2000). For, whatever the complexity required, the point of public-sphere theory is to generate principles whereby the *adequacy* of current forms of public consultation and deliberation can be judged in relation to the decision-making processes that concern them. Nancy Fraser's essay on 'Transnationalizing the Public Sphere' asks, afresh, whether *any* version of public-sphere theory (Habermas's original model, Habermas's recent networked model, or accounts generated from critiques of Habermas's models) performs the critical job we expect of it. Fraser thus takes the normative/concrete tension inherent in public-sphere debate to a new level. But do her particular formulations of that tension offer the most

productive way of addressing the deep problems to which
she has helpfully drawn attention?

I approach this question as a sociologist of culture and
media. For me the value of public-sphere theory has been
not that it offers a model which fits in any simple way with
actually existing democracies, and media institutions' role
within them, but that, against the background of public
debate excessively influenced by market naturalism, it insists
that something fundamental to our democracies *is* at stake
in how public discussion and political structures interrelate,
and that we *do* have normative reference-points from which
to evaluate the operations of powerful political, corporate,
and media actors as they affect those interrelations. The task
of public-sphere theory has recently become much harder:
transnationalizing pressures create a disjuncture between
theory and actuality that, as Fraser indicates, must be
urgently addressed.

Fraser's strategy is to re-scale the public-sphere concept,
clarifying how the key tests – of normative legitimacy and
political efficacy – would apply to such a transnational public
sphere: How can we establish that those who would need to
be included *are* fairly included and that the resulting space
of debate has effective influence over the *relevant* decisions?
This strategy, while it raises crucial questions of long-term
interest, may (in the short term) risk focusing our attention
on a problem (how might a new fully transnational public
sphere be built?) that is under current conditions insoluble,
while diverting us from the points within *existing* national
and local public spheres where pressures of transnationalization need to and can, more plausibly, be addressed. Instead,
should we aim for something more modest already suggested
by Fraser's title: that is, an account of what it would be to
transnation*alize* existing public spheres?

My argument will involve making distinctions between
the six presuppositions, all tied to a Westphalian model of
nation-states, on which Fraser argues public-sphere theory
to date has depended. Fraser outlines transnationalizing
processes which disrupt each of these presuppositions. But

are they equally far advanced for each presupposition? If yes, then, because *all* the presuppositions of the public sphere have been disrupted, there is no choice but to rethink its basis completely. But if not, it may be productive to try another approach: rather than attempting to define the conditions for a wholly new public sphere on a transnational scale, we can investigate, first, how transnationalizing pressures might be more adequately addressed in public spheres on *every* level (including local and national), and, second, whether an eventual 'transnational public sphere' might be better understood not as a single thing, but as the networked resultant of transformations at multiple levels. That will be my strategy in this essay.

Fraser's Formulation of the Problem with Existing Public-Sphere Theory

Let me begin by summarizing the problem with existing public-sphere theory as Fraser sees it, bringing out the particular way she sets out to solve the problem she identifies.

As Fraser clarifies, public-sphere theory is not a descriptive model which works well as long as its elements track the detailed mechanisms of existing democratic states; the purpose of public-sphere theory is normative, to assess whether existing structures provide the *right, not the wrong*, group of people (all of those affected by a set of decisions) the opportunity to participate *effectively, not trivially*, in the formulation and implementation of those decisions. Within discourse ethics this relates to an underlying principle that Seyla Benhabib expresses thus: '[T]he basic idea behind [Habermas's] model is that only those norms can be said to be valid . . . which would be agreed to by all those affected by their consequences', reaching a decision in a satisfactory way (1996: 70). It follows that the conditions of normative legitimacy and political efficacy are not incidental, or subsidiary, features of public-sphere theory's application to the world, but preconditions for that application having *any point at all*. For all the force of the detailed critiques of

Habermas's theory to date, most, Fraser argues, including her own, have been grounded, like the theory itself, within assumptions about the Westphalian state which no longer simply hold. As a result, the efficacy and value of public-sphere theory are fundamentally challenged.

Habermas's later complexification of public-sphere theory (in *Between Facts and Norms*) does not escape this problem. Here is Habermas isolating the working assumptions on which his networked model of the public sphere depends:

> The distinction between normal and extraordinary modes of posing and solving problems . . . can be rendered fruitful for a sociological translation and realistic interpretation of the discourse concept of democracy *only if we introduce two further assumptions*. The *illegitimate independence* of social and administrative power vis-à-vis democratically generated communicative power is averted to the extent that the periphery has both (a) a specific set of capabilities and (b) sufficient occasion to exercise them. The first assumption, (a), refers to the capacities to ferret out, identify, and effectively thematize latent problems of social integration (which require political solutions); moreover an active periphery *must then introduce them* via parliamentary (or judicial) sluices into the political system *in a way that disrupts the latter's routines*. . . . Resonant and autonomous public spheres of this sort [on the periphery of Habermas's new networked public sphere] must in turn be anchored in the voluntary associations of civil society and embedded in liberal patterns of political culture and socialization; in a word, they depend on a rationalized lifeworld that meets them halfway. (1996: 358, my emphasis)

Habermas goes on to explore the conditions for this happening in terms of a relation between politics and everyday life:

> The political public sphere can fulfil its function of perceiving and thematizing encompassing social problems only insofar as it develops out of the communication taking place among those who are potentially affected. It is carried by *a*

public recruited from the entire citizenry. (1996: 365, my
emphasis)

Two things are striking here. First, Habermas emphasizes
that the normative problem for democratic workings is the
'illegitimate independence' of administrative power from
political power (with its ultimate popular roots), thus a way
must be found of meshing the two together so that everyday
communication ultimately finds a route by which to 'disrupt
the political system's routines': I will return to this vital point
in my conclusion. Second, even after posing the problem so
vividly, Habermas solves it in terms that take no account of
the limits of the Westphalian model: there is no other way
of interpreting the phrase 'entire citizenry' except as invoking a national citizenship. Indeed Habermas's recent discussion of a possible European public sphere defines it in terms
of a network for '*citizens* of all member states' (2001: 17, my
emphasis). So those who might be relevant to everyday communication who are not formal citizens of the territory considered are, by definition, excluded from the conversation.
This, as Fraser points out, is deeply problematic.

How, then, does Fraser set out to solve this problem? She
breaks it down into a consideration, one by one, of the six
specific presuppositions on which the Westphalian version
of the public sphere depends. Those presuppositions can
be distinguished, I suggest, into three contrasting sorts:
first, there is a presupposition *of intent* (presupposition (1)
in Fraser's essay), which ties the overall aim of a public
sphere to the reform of its associated territory: so the aim
of the classic public sphere is 'the democratization of the
modern territorial (nation-)state', 'critiquing . . . the democratic deficits of actually existing Westphalian states' (pp. 13
and 14, this volume). Second, there are what we might call
identifying presuppositions (listed as (2) and (3) in Fraser's
essay), which identify the participants or appropriate topics
of debate in a national public sphere: that is, the nation-
state's citizen-members and the regulation of its economic
and social arrangements. Then there are *infrastructural*

presuppositions (listed as (4)–(6) by Fraser), which deal with the cultural means by which a public sphere so motivated and constituted is sustained – a national media infrastructure, operating in an assumed single national language, on the basis of a national cultural tradition of argumentation and debate. In spite of my distinctions between these presuppositions, Fraser's aim is to show that public spheres today are 'increasingly transnational or postnational' in relation to all six presuppositions (p. 26, this volume).

This way of formulating the problem with public-sphere theory is open to two objections. The first, an empirical objection (see next section), is that Fraser exaggerates the degree to which those infrastructural presuppositions have in fact been rendered outdated. The second objection (to be discussed immediately) is theoretical: *Does Fraser's way of setting up the problem privilege one type of solution at the expense of other possible solutions?* More specifically, does Fraser privilege as a solution the building of an entirely new public sphere on a transnational scale at the expense of considering an alternative solution: that is, one achieved through the linkage of multiple spaces on a variety of scales, each transformed by transnationalizing pressures, no doubt, but articulated together in a new way that does not produce a single space at all?

Without question we need 'a public sphere' that *in some way* is aimed at the activities of a political space larger than the nation-state (the presupposition of 'intent') and we need 'a public sphere' whose workings *in some way* incorporate both people beyond the nation citizenry and issues whose scope exceeds that of the nation-state (the 'identifying' presuppositions). But it does not follow from this that the only way of meeting these needs is through one single, continuous space or entity that operates on a different scale from the Westphalian nation-state. More specifically, it does not follow that the only way to satisfy the problems with the presuppositions of intent and identification is to create a public sphere whose *cultural infrastructure* is 'transnational', in other words a fully 'transnational public sphere'. Why not make Habermas's idea of a networked public sphere more radical, applying its principle of distribution not just within the space of the nation, or a larger but still unitary space extending beyond the nation, but to produce a more adequate linkage between many different public spheres operating on different scales, local, national, regional, even global? This, I take it, is part of what James Bohman (2007) suggests through his concept of 'democracy *across* borders'.

But this more radically distributed solution to the 'transnational problem' is not allowed for in Fraser's account. So when she identifies the infrastructure of the communicative contemporary public sphere, she writes only of 'current flows of transnational publicity':[4] what about national and local publicity? And when she proposes solutions to the problem, she argues that public-sphere theory must now address not one, but two (implicitly separate) levels, with the new problems arising only in addressing the second:

> A critical conception [of the public sphere] *can no longer restrict* its attention to the direction of communicative flows in established polities, where publicity should constrain an already known and constituted addressee. *In addition*, it must consider the need to construct new addresses for public opinion, in the sense of new, transnational public powers that possess the administrative capacity to solve transnational problems. (p. 33, this volume, emphases added)

Fraser's two-level formulation leaves no room for a different transformation: the addressing of the 'already known and constituted addressee' in a new way, through deliberations involving an adjusted version of the original group of participants, operating through an adjusted version of the national cultural infrastructure. Fraser's weighting of her argument towards one, more drastic solution matters if it excludes from consideration adjustments that are easier to imagine than the construction of a completely new addressee.

The Limits of Transnational Publicity

Let me now evaluate Fraser's empirical starting-point: *Have in fact all of the presuppositions of the public-sphere model been disrupted by transnationalization to the degree that she supposes?*

In discussing the 'where' of public-sphere communication, Fraser says this is no longer a 'national communications infrastructure' (presumably old-style print and broadcasting), but 'deterritorialized cyberspace'. Yet, in the case of the UK, TV (which is largely TV addressed to a UK audience) remains the main news source for 65 per cent of the population, while the internet is the main news source for only 6 per cent (Ofcom 2007: Figure 3.1); while hours watching terrestrial news still (at nearly two hours per week) dwarf those spent on internet news sites (just over an hour a month), by a multiple of eight (Ofcom 2007: Figure 3.4 and Table A2.26).[5] Overall UK TV viewing was *unchanged* between 2002 and 2007 (Ofcom 2007–8). While exactly comparative European figures are difficult to obtain, in Germany in 2008, 76.5 per cent still used TV daily for news, compared with 14.9 per cent for the internet (Oemichen and Schröter 2008: Table 9), and overall TV viewing *rose* (from 214 to 225 minutes daily) between 2002 and 2007.[6] So these statistics are hardly evidence of a shift to deterritorialized *cyberspace*, even if (which I doubt) we should accept that cyberspace *is* deterritorialized: again we should note that, after social networking sites, YouTube and eBay, the BBC is by some margin the most searched-for brand for UK internet users according to the latest available figures (Hitwise 2009: 5).

Fraser also makes an argument for drastic change in relation to the language-base of the public sphere. Certainly there are issues about how, in Britain, for example, the parallel worlds of English and, say, Polish or Arabic media can be linked up. This is hardly happening at the moment, and needs to be developed. But this does not require us to put all our efforts into imagining, in place of Britain's dominant English-language public sphere, a public sphere that is overall multilingual, an extremely difficult undertaking.

More generally, if we think about the public sphere sociologically, as a process underpinned by habits of media use in everyday life, these habits remain, and are likely to remain, largely *national, not transnational*, in their focus. In the Public Connection project on which I worked at the London School of Economics with Sonia Livingstone and Tim Markham between 2003 and 2006, we found, contrary to expectation, little evidence that people were oriented either to media or to public worlds beyond the national or the local (Couldry et al. 2007). That is not to say that national and local public spheres are not, in new ways, porous to transnational pressures, only that habits of media consumption are not simply determined by those new possibilities.

None of this is accidental or aberrant. On the contrary, the systems that actually regulate *everyday* life (taxes, border controls, rights to start a business, criminal law) still *issue* in large part from the nation-state and not from a transnational power source, even if transnational powers set the parameters within which national states can act in these domains; and they still get implemented often at a *local* level. So why should transnationalizing pressures not continue to be best challenged, initially at least, within national and local public spheres?

If Fraser is incorrect in claiming that all the presuppositions of the public-sphere model have become invalid at once, then there is no obvious advantage in imagining the public sphere to be rebuilt *de novo* on some other scale, targeted at another addressee and populated by a differently constituted group of citizens. Indeed, as we move beyond an exclusively Westphalian understanding of the political processes that the public sphere aims to regulate, the nation-state may remain crucial to that transformation.

From the Transnational Public Sphere to Transnationalized Public Spheres

Arguably, then, restoring public-sphere theory's critical edge involves not only in the longer term imagining a completely new object, a public sphere on a transnational scale, but also more immediately answering a different question: *What would it be to transnationalize the local and national public spheres within what are still largely national media infrastructures, cultures that are still relatively homogeneous linguistically, and historical traditions of political engagement that till now have been, but arguably no longer should remain, exclusively limited to contributions from national citizens?* This would apply Fraser's most radical proposal – her reworking of the 'all-affected' principle in terms not of the default position of a national citizen-body but of a broader understanding of 'co-imbrication' in political, social, and economic processes that cross borders – to *existing* public spheres. Let me develop these thoughts a little further.

Fraser talks throughout the essay about a 'transnation*al* public sphere', but her title 'Transnationalizing the Public Sphere' is compatible with a different term: the transnation-al*ized* public sphere (*or spheres*). This might seem a minor semantic difference, but it is not. Transnationalizing pressures, I am suggesting, create two quite different types of challenge for democratic politics: a challenge of *extension*, so that decisions increasingly need to be made, and public opinion starts to need to be formed, across much larger spaces than before (addressed potentially by something we might call a transnational public sphere, separately identifiable from national or local public spheres); and a challenge *of intensity*, so that what counts *as* a national or local issue needs itself to be rethought as our awareness of the interdependence of local actions and translocal forces increases. This second challenge – of intensity – introduces a transnational dimension into the most local of acts, and so requires that *every* public sphere at *any* scale becomes amenable to influences, voices, cultural norms, and media inputs that do not fit within the implied boundaries of the Westphalian model. We might fear that this entirely 'unstitches' the fabric of the public sphere at the national and local levels. Alternatively, we can imagine it as *enriching* the fabric of national and local public spheres, in the process *re-forming* national and local citizens into a larger group of actors with a sensitivity to transnational processes and demands, thereby perhaps making imaginable more effective long-term political mechanisms on a transnational scale.

On the level of individual practice, some such transformations are already under way. Think of the choices we make at a supermarket aisle about whether to buy local produce or produce flown in from across the world; think of our choice whether or not to buy a cheap sandwich whose low price, it may turn out, depends on the exploitation of migrant workers in an illegal factory just a few miles from where we live; think of people going to work in the knowledge that their job may depend not only on management decisions made far away, but also on national or local government's willingness to treat distant 'market-based' decisions as open to 'political' intervention or something beyond the bounds of political challenge. Some of these choices are beginning to be recognizable as part of politics; others, as yet, are not. But they are all examples of how transnational forces potentially shift the boundaries of the political on every scale.

It is here – staying within the national and local scale – that critical public-sphere theory, and particularly Fraser's rethinking of the 'all-affected' principle, immediately cuts into contemporary practice. This connects with other critical reflections on contemporary democracy: the need for what Pierre Rosanvallon calls new 'acts and discourses for producing commonality' (2007: 250) at all levels, including local politics; and indeed Fraser's separate work on the injustices in the framing of politics (2005) at all levels.

If we consider the case of migrant workers who move from poorer to richer economies, resolving the issues of regulation, legal rights, and justice is impossible within the confines of an individual state. Yet the resulting issues of justice, fair treatment, resources, and recognition generally arise first at national, indeed local, levels. However, migrants rarely appear as political or social actors in Britain's public sphere, important though they are to its national and local economies: a rare and impressive exception, outside the normal range of daily media, was Ken Loach's film *It's a Free World* (2007), about Polish migrant workers in London.

How should we think about the implications of this paradigmatic case? It may imply that migrant workers should have a voice, in some way, in the organization of resources and the taking of decisions in the localities where they make a sustained contribution to the economy and social provision. This is already a major change from the present circumstances; to respond to it would require a major rethinking of existing local and national public spheres.

It may also imply a wider principle, that anyone (wherever they are) affected by an international issue (in this case the rules governing migration of labour and their application) should be represented in any decisions on the adoption or implementation of those rules. This second possibility would seem to be implied by Fraser's argument to replace the 'citizenship test' as a short-cut to addressing the 'all-affected' principle by a different principle of 'co-imbrication' in 'a common set of . . . life-conditioning structures whose effects are at issue' (p. 30, this volume). But specifying all the groups across the world 'affected' by issues such as global labour markets (or indeed the global economy or global warming) would be very difficult; prima facie *everyone* is affected in some way or other. And imagining a communications infrastructure that would enable this huge group to talk and be heard where it matters is even more difficult, not to say impossible, owing to its complexity. This is not to say that transnational debate (international NGOs, etc.) is irrelevant to such issues – one can easily imagine an international campaign online making a significant difference on any level where such issues are discussed. But within the current political infrastructure, it seems too difficult to imagine how to constitute a public sphere that reflects on a transnational scale the interest of all world citizens in the many issues raised by transnational migration and labour.

More practical in the immediate term is to consider how the quality of local and national spheres might be transnationalized, influencing *national* decision processes, and through them indirectly international decision-making processes. The local press, for example, might be encouraged to show greater sensitivity to a range of local populations: Polish migrant workers in the UK (in towns such as Reading) have local Polish newspapers, but that is not the same as their interests and voices being more adequately represented elsewhere in local or national public spheres. Don't the voices of migrant workers in Britain, and indeed their families abroad who depend on their remitted income, need to be heard more in British media than at present? How often are they represented other than in stereotyped, hostile form?

This is not just a matter of better rules or regulations. It is something more fundamental: a matter, as Étienne Balibar writes, of putting the term 'community of citizens' 'back into action' so that its recognition enables us to take into account 'the contribution of all those who are present . . . in [a] social space' (2004: 50). Without doubt, Nancy Fraser's essay challenges us to move in this direction.

Conclusion

My aim has not been to give up on Fraser's insistence that we need to rescue the critical edge of public-sphere theory. Only on the basis of such theory are we impelled to ask: *Do the transnationalized public spheres just envisaged involve all the right people? Are they effective in the right places?* And to what extent do our answers to those first two questions *require also* a separate transnational public sphere that *supplements* the national and local public spheres and addresses political entities formed on scales beyond the national? If they do, then the problems Fraser raises about the constitution of that supplementary, newly located public sphere return. Insofar also as the international hegemony of neoliberal discourse *trumps* national and local deliberation in particular places, there *is* a democratic deficit (Habermas 2001), which even transnationalized national and local public spheres must address.

This leads to an underlying problem whose urgency Fraser suggests, but which is unresolved in any version of public-sphere theory: How should we understand the *articulation* of public-sphere theory to the conditions under which existing democracies work? While Slavko Splichal (2009) is right that public-sphere theory itself cannot define the conditions under which the 'public' formally influence government (a matter for political science and democratic theory), there is a problem if existing public spheres conform, say, to Habermas's networked model, yet work in ways of which national governments take little account, as Aeron Davis (2009: 289–94) argues for the UK case.

What is the underlying notion of articulation between public-sphere and political decision-making (distinct from formal political influence) that gives sense to public-sphere theory? Here we reach the boundary of what that theory specifies; since this articulation is not internal to the public sphere itself, it has remained little discussed. In earlier versions it was based on an implicit condition of *resonance*: discussions in the London coffee house could be *assumed* to matter to the UK state because they circulated, gathered momentum, were reworked and refashioned, in a word 'resonated', within a space whose boundaries for most purposes were coterminous with the space that determined the actions of that state, the UK's bounded national territory. But such resonance becomes more difficult to assume when both the flow of public discussion and the pressures which shape state actions spill beyond national borders. The deep risk that transnationalizing pressures pose for the public sphere as a practical concept is that neither citizen discourse nor the networks of political action are *ever* focused in such a way that they are heard in dialogue with each other.

Our best starting-point for addressing this risk, I have argued, is not to fall short in imagining a transnational public sphere we do not yet know, but to consider what it would mean to transnationalize the public spheres we do know. That leads to an issue neglected by Fraser, but also not answered here: how to move away from the idea that each public sphere has an exclusive citizen constituency towards a notion of overlapping constituencies whose mutual interactions require regulation in ways that have not yet been clarified. How, in other words, can we rethink for a world of increased complexity the conditions under which public opinion at any level is adequately articulated with the scales of political action?

Notes

Thanks to my Goldsmiths colleague Aeron Davis and Slavko Splichal of the University of Ljubljana for stimulating discussions and access to their recent writings which helped me clarify my argument.

1 Compare Habermas 1996: 362 (on media) with Peters 1993 and Thompson 1993.
2 Compare Habermas 1996: 354–5 with Fraser 1992.
3 Habermas 1996: 360.
4 As when she writes: 'Unless we can envision conditions under which current flows of transnational publicity could conceivably become legitimate and efficacious . . .' (p. 27, this volume).
5 In the Netherlands, the multiple was almost as high (6.8, based on an average of 46.7 minutes per day spent on consuming television news and 6.9 minutes a day spent on internet-derived news). Source: Mediamonitor 2009: *http://www.mediamonitor.nl*. Thanks to Irene Costera Meijer for alerting me to this Dutch source.
6 Source: Medien Basisdaten: *http://www.ard.de/intern/basisdaten/onlinenutzung/* (last accessed 20 November 2008, no longer available online). Thanks to Andreas Hepp and Jeffrey Wimmer for supplying me with these and other German statistics.

References

Balibar, É. (2004) *We The People of Europe?* Princeton: Princeton University Press.

Benhabib, S. (1996) 'Toward a Deliberative Model of Democratic Legitimacy', in S. Benhabib (ed.), *Democracy and Difference.* Princeton: Princeton University Press.

Bohman, J. (2007) *Democracy across Borders: From Demos to Demoi.* Cambridge, MA: MIT Press.

Couldry, N., S. Livingstone, and T. Markham (2007) *Media Consumption and Public Engagement: Beyond the Presumption of Attention.* Basingstoke: Palgrave.

Curran, J. (2000) 'Rethinking Media and Democracy', in J. Curran and M. Gurevitch (eds), *Mass Media and Society,* 3rd edn. London: Arnold.

Davis, A. (2009) 'Evaluating Communication in the British Parliamentary Public Sphere', *British Journal of Politics and International Relations* 11: 280–97.

Fraser, N. (1992) 'Rethinking the Public Sphere: A Contribution to the Critique of Actually Existing Democracy', in C. Calhoun (ed.), *Habermas and the Public Sphere.* Cambridge, MA: MIT Press.

Fraser, N. (2005) 'Reframing Justice in a Globalizing World', *New Left Review* 36(Nov.–Dec.): 69–88.

Habermas, J. (1996) *Between Facts and Norms: Contributions to a Discourse Theory of Law and Democracy,* trans. W. Rehg. Cambridge: Polity.

Habermas, J. (2001) 'Why Europe Needs a Constitution', *New Left Review* 11 (Sept.–Oct.): http://newleftreview.org/II/11/jurgen-habermas-why-europe-needs-a-constitution (accessed 4 November 2013).

Hitwise (2009) *UK Online Media Roundup,* March: http://www.hitwise.co.uk.

Oemichen E. and C. Schröter (2008) 'Medienübergreifende Nutzungsmuster:
Struktur- und Funktionsverschiebungen', *Media Perspektiven* 8: 394–405.

Ofcom (2007) *New News, Future News,* June: http://stakeholders.ofcom.org.uk/market-data-research/other/tv-research/newnews/ (accessed 8 November 2013).

Ofcom (2007–8) *Public Service Broadcasting Reports:* http://stakeholders.ofcom.org.uk/broadcasting/reviews-investigations/

public-service-broadcasting/annrep/ (accessed 8 November 2013).

Peters, J.D. (1993) 'Distrust of Representation: Habermas on the Public Sphere', *Media Culture & Society* 15(4): 541–71.

Rosanvallon, P. (2007) *Democracy Past and Future*. New York: Columbia University Press.

Splichal, S. (2009) ' "New Media", "Old" Theories: Does the (National) Public Melt into the Air of Global Governance?', *European Journal of Communication* 24(4): 391–405.

Thompson, J. (1993) 'The Theory of the Public Sphere', *Theory, Culture & Society* 10(3): 174–89.

3

Towards Transnational Democratization?

Kate Nash

Critical theorists analyse emancipatory possibilities and normative ideals that are significant in reality, testing them in thought, and elaborating guidelines for political practice. In 'Transnationalizing the Public Sphere', Nancy Fraser analyses the possibility of the 'public sphere' beyond the national frame. The characteristic clarity of Fraser's thinking makes for an important contribution to debate in this area. She examines assumptions that a global public sphere already exists, and argues that, as it is so vital to any possibility of postnational democracy, we need to be absolutely clear about how we are using the concept. Building on Habermas's work on the structuration of the national public sphere, she argues that to be relevant to democracy a public sphere must involve: (i) normative legitimacy – it must enable democratic discussion between 'all affected' by a particular issue; and (ii) political efficacy – a transnational public sphere must influence, or even form, accountable political institutions that act for 'all affected' through binding law and administration.

In the spirit of critical-theoretical questioning of the identities, institutions, and norms that are required by democracy beyond the national frame, I will raise a number of questions concerning, firstly, the requirement of normative legitimacy, which seems to me to be problematic conceptually in the Habermasian tradition, and, secondly, Fraser's understanding of political efficacy. Although I share Fraser's view that normative ideals are vital to assessing 'actually existing democracy', I think the conditions required by the Habermasian theory of the public sphere are too demanding to be of use to already existing forms of transnational political action. 'Transnational advocacy networks' (TANs) are far from legitimate in Fraser's terms, and they are indeed far from sufficient for global democracy. Nevertheless, I will argue that there is a way of understanding TANs as democratizing, though not democratic. Analysing what I take to be implicit in Fraser's theorization of democracy as involving counterpublic spheres, the notion of 'usefulness', I argue that it helps us understand 'actually existing' possibilities for democratizing global governance today.

Normative Legitimacy: *The* Public?

In *The Structural Transformation of the Public Sphere* (1989), Habermas conceives of the bourgeois public sphere as a unified space in which citizens engaged in largely face-to-face, rational critical discussion in order to discover and refine the universal principles that should guide the state for the common good. In his subsequent work on the public sphere, especially in *Between Facts and Norms* (1996), Habermas has significantly revised this understanding in response to critics and in order to develop a theory of the public sphere which is better suited to contemporary societies. In particular he has taken note of feminist critics who have pointed to the exclusions of the historically dominant public sphere and developed understandings of the continuing relevance of what Fraser (1997) calls 'counterpublic spheres', which do not rely on rationalist argument to influence government, which may actually be partially integrated into the state itself (where they are 'strong'), and which articulate claims to justice of particular groups and communities (see also Calhoun 1992; Landes 1998). In addition, Habermas has revised his view of the 'refeudalization' of the public sphere, which he saw as resulting from capitalist industrialization. He now understands the mass media to be crucial to any functioning of the public sphere in modern societies. Media representations, whilst always susceptible to the influence of money and power, are not wholly determined by economic and political interests. Indeed, they are embedded in strategies of interpretation and reinterpretation and are therefore subject to criticism and to redefinition on the part of media audiences, who are not passive 'cultural dopes'. In his more recent work, then, rather than the ideal of rational deliberation between members of a face-to-face, singular, and unified public, Habermas sees 'popular sovereignty [as] no longer embodied in a visibly identified gathering of autonomous citizens. It pulls back into the, as it were, "subjectless" forms of communication circulating through forums and legislative bodies' (1996: 136). Organizations and movements of civil society which 'distill and transmit [how societal problems resonate in the private life spheres] in amplified form to the public sphere' (1996: 367) are especially important in these forms of communication.

Habermas now understands 'the' public sphere as both unified and plural, though his theoretical focus is on its plurality. He sees it as a highly complex network made up of differentiated social spaces in which public opinion is formed and tested for generalizability on various levels, from the 'episodic' publics of street politics, through the 'occasional' publics of staged events, up to the 'abstract' public sphere of isolated readers, listeners, and viewers in the mass media (Habermas 1996: 373–4). For Habermas, these different publics remain 'porous to one another'. But do they therefore constitute a single unified public sphere, as suggested by his continued use of '*the*' public sphere? What authorizes this 'the'? In his earlier understanding, it was structured by a kind of will towards rational consensus. How is 'the' public sphere unified in Habermas's revised theory?

Empirically, it seems that, on occasion, there is a relatively unified 'mediated public' (Thompson 1995). We can say that 'porousness' works to enable the circulation and formation of public opinion across a wide range of sites where there is similarity of *content* in how news stories are reported (in different newspapers, on websites, in broadcasts, etc.). In my study of the cultural politics of human rights, for example, I found that although consensus was never reached in the US press over what to do with prisoners in Guantánamo Bay, there was a degree of unity in the content of the debates on the topic in that similar arguments concerning the prisoners' status, and how they should be treated and tried, were rehearsed across a range of newspapers (Nash 2009). There are other occasions on which it seems likely that a relative unity will be achieved: in cases of political scandal, for example, or highly successful pro- or anti-war campaigning. But in relation to many other issues, the media are likely to be polarized between opposing factions (as on abortion in the US, for example), with virtually no dialogue between them. Or stories and viewpoints are rehearsed amongst those who have a direct stake in debates, and largely ignored elsewhere – as with the details of financial dealings, which (before the financial crisis) were covered in the financial press, and very little elsewhere, even in the 'quality' media. Much 'foreign' news, too, is simply ignored by popular media, except where it concerns disasters or crises, or where national citizens are caught up in events.

If not through the form (reason) or the content of deliberations, then, how might we understand the unity of 'the' public sphere? Perhaps Habermas allows himself to assume this unity as a product of what Fraser refers to as the limitations of the Westphalian political imaginary. He imagines 'the' public sphere as unified as it is linked to 'the' territorially bounded state. There appears to be nothing that *necessarily* or routinely unifies communication in what might rather be thought of as a *multiplicity* of public spheres (even if empirically they may be relatively unified on occasion) *except* that they are in some way oriented towards, even bound to, a single state.

But does the unity of the public sphere remain important for the normative aspect of Habermas's theory of democracy? There is no doubt that the theory of democracy he sets out in *Between Facts and Norms* is much more sophisticated than his earlier understanding of the public sphere, and much better suited to the complexities of the societies in which we live. But while it is more realistic as sociological theory, in terms of the ideals against which democracy should be assessed, it seems that something has been lost. It is unclear how 'subjectless' forms of communication can be legitimate as an expression of 'popular sovereignty' if citizens have not actually deliberated together. In Habermas's revised theory of democracy, the '*social* level of institutionalized processes of deliberation and decision-making', that is, the judiciary and legislature of the liberal-democratic state, has a new significance (Habermas 1996: 461–2). It seems to be in these institutions that the normative legitimacy of democratic decision-making, which ultimately depends on rational deliberation, is secured. The influence of the mediated public sphere appears to be important in this model of democracy principally insofar as it raises issues and makes social problems visible. They are then deliberated on and conflicts are resolved in ways that are justifiable in universal terms within the law-making and administrative institutions of the constitutional state. Some civil society organizations may be directly involved in these deliberations, but the great majority of the citizenry will not participate.

There is surely a problem here, however, in terms of the legitimacy of any resulting legal judgement, legislation, or policy. If there is no unified public sphere in which citizens actually deliberate with each other, but only multiple and diverse public spheres that influence *what* is deliberated on in state institutions without affecting *how* the content of debates is framed, how are policies and legislation legitimate? They may be rationally defended in universalist terms *in principle*, but in practice there is no way of knowing what relationship decisions have to what citizens actually think, know, or believe to be the case. Without real, society-wide processes of deliberation in which different social groups debate agreements and disagreements, and learn to shift their views of public interest as a result, elite decision-making cannot be informed by citizens' reflections on interests and values. In such a case, where deliberation across political divisions is not actually possible in 'the' public sphere, what we have may just as well be understood as a hegemonic universalizing of particular claims and interests rather than as consensus on universal principles agreed on as a result of rational deliberation (see Norval 2007).

Clearly, as Fraser argues in 'Transnationalizing the Public Sphere', if we try to 'scale up' Habermas's model of the public sphere beyond the national level, what is most obviously missing is that transnational discussions on matters which affect people beyond national borders do not take place within a bounded political space with mechanisms whereby public influence may be translated into law-making and administration. Prior to this problem, however, it seems to me that there is a deeper conceptual problem with Habermas's view of 'subjectless' popular sovereignty as democratic. In fact, thinking about 'scaling up' this model demonstrates that the problem with this conception of the public sphere is conceptual not empirical. The absence of state-like structures through which the influence of public spheres might be realized at the transnational level enables us to see more clearly that once we lose the idea of *a* unified public sphere which produces well-discussed consensus to influence *a* state, we also lose the normative value of the Rousseauian notion of 'popular sovereignty' as will formation. But the problem is not one of scale *per se*. It is much older: Given the complexity of contemporary societies, how might we conceive of democracy in terms of popular will formation that is genuinely inclusive and genuinely for the common good? Habermas's solution, strongly influenced by Fraser's work on counterpublic spheres, is a solution to the problem of complexity and inclusivity. It is not, however, a solution to the perennial problem of democratic will formation in complex societies. Nor is it a solution to the problem of how society may be regulated for the benefit of all where 'all affected' participate in 'giving the law to themselves'.

Efficacy as 'Usefulness'

Turning now to the second criterion Fraser outlines as necessary to a democratic public sphere, the question of political
efficacy, we also turn to more empirical matters. In her
analysis of the possibility of a transnational public sphere,
Fraser makes the important point that the national public
sphere developed in a setting in which relative state control
over the capitalist economy came *before* democratization in
forms of class compromise. She is equally clear that, although
there are overlapping institutions and organizations of global
governance, at the global level there is no agency comparable
to the European state of the eighteenth century in relation
to which Habermas theorized the bourgeois public sphere.
Fraser implies, then, that at the transnational level, legitimate public spheres must *both* establish the capacity of effective institutions *and* at the same time translate public opinion
into law and administration, to bring effective pressure to
bear on those institutions. In other words, in contrast to the
national public sphere, post-Westphalian public spheres must
both enable the conditions for open participation in wide-
ranging public debate *and* at the same time create effective
but porous and responsive global institutions.

At the global scale there is clearly nothing that resembles
a world state (which is generally considered to be a good
thing), and neither, as Fraser has so convincingly argued, is
there anything like a global public sphere judged in terms of
Habermas's theory of democracy. What has become increasingly important over the last few decades, however, is the
emergence and enormous growth of the NGO sector in relation to intergovernmental organizations (IGOs), especially
the United Nations, and including the International Monetary Fund and the World Bank. What implications does this
development have for democracy beyond the national frame?
Here I will first consider the extent to which the transnational networks in which NGOs are embedded can be analysed in the terms of Fraser's own criticism and adaptation
of Habermas's democratic theory in terms of 'counterpublic

spheres'. I will then go on to discuss how, in my view, Fraser also expanded Habermas's concept of 'efficacy' in her work on counterpublic spheres, and to suggest that it is equally important to do so in relation to postnational democracy.

In 'Rethinking the Public Sphere' (1997), Fraser argues that democratic society is best understood in terms of over-lapping public spheres. The main example she discusses is the feminist movement, but she stresses that her argument is equally applicable to what were once known as 'new social movements' generally: anti-racist, gay and lesbian, environ-mental, and so on. What Fraser calls 'subaltern counterpub-lics' are constituted as challenging the norms and assumptions of the mainstream public sphere, adopting alternative ways of mobilizing public opinion, and often also alternative modes of participation that are decidedly not intended to be rational, nor to subsume particular group interests in order to support a hegemonic understanding of the 'common good' that favours the privileged. In addition, and more controver-sially, Fraser argues that counterpublic spheres are most effective when they are strong: when they involve both opinion formation and decision-making. This is controver-sial in that 'new social movements' were often seen, and even defined in contrast to 'interest groups', as mobilizing in civil society rather than as addressing the state (see Melucci 1989). In contrast, Fraser argues, 'strong public spheres' are more effective; movements that work directly to influence govern-ment decision-making in parliaments or local decision-making bodies will be more successful in transforming society than those that confine themselves to persuasion and direct action in civil society (Fraser 1997: 89–92).

Where they exist, transnational social movements (TSMs) resemble counterpublic spheres in analytic terms. They are similar in that they produce knowledge and contest ortho-doxies in mainstream society, often using spectacular and popular forms of address and innovative political action. A good example is Castells' detailed analysis of the movement against climate change, which involves scientists and celebri-ties, professional NGOs and influential individuals like Al

Gore, detailed scientific arguments that can only be understood by experts, and apocalyptic scenarios that capture the
imagination of novelists and film-makers (Castells 2009:
303–39). Of course, TSMs are additionally complex because
of the multi-scalar setting in which they work. It is multi-
scalar in that, as well as addressing members of civil societies
and states 'from below', they direct their efforts towards
IGOs, sometimes trying to influence their policies and frame-
works specifically, sometimes trying to put pressure on states
'from above' as well as 'from below' (see Keck and Sikkink
1988a; Risse et al. 1999; Tarrow 2005). To the extent that
they are able to act as such, TSMs are 'strong' counterpublic
spheres, directly addressing policy-making and legislation
from within IGOs and states as well as stimulating discussion and dissent in civil society.

It is important to note, however, that in practical terms it
is extremely difficult to mobilize TSMs. NGOs are much
more commonly embedded in 'transnational advocacy networks' (TANs) rather than transnational social movements.
According to Keck and Sikkink, TANs are defined as
'includ[ing] those relevant actors working internationally
on an issue, who are bound together by shared values, a
common discourse, and dense exchanges of information and
services' (1998a: 3). TANs are *sometimes* linked to transnational or to national social movements. According to Tarrow,
what distinguishes TSMs is that they are clearly (the implica-
tion here is 'deeply') rooted in networks in more than one
state, and are engaged in continuous, not episodic, engagement with at least one state. Rather than 'reaching out' for
support beyond the state, they are *intrinsically* connected
across borders (Tarrow 2001). Whilst Keck and Sikkink
(1998b) *assume* that TANs tend to be sustained by social
movements, the relationship between these two different
forms is rather a conceptual and empirical *question* in each
case. According to Tarrow, achieving and maintaining a
TSM is extremely difficult compared to creating and maintaining a TAN. This is understandable if we consider that
the latter consist of professional workers in NGOs and IGOs

for whom building networks is a paid job and, more often than not, a career.

TANs, like TSMs, share some of the features of 'counter-public spheres'. Again, they work principally through challenging and forming opinion. Indeed, the use of emotion, especially 'shaming' those who neglect or actively suppress discussion of issues of importance, is a well-known feature of this type of political action: members of TANs do not confine themselves to rational deliberation in order to persuade (Keck and Sikkink 1998a). However, TANs are oriented towards influencing policy change in and through IGOs; their principal efforts are not directed towards the production and contestation of knowledge and opinion as such, and trying to influence policy change indirectly through civil society is not their most important tactic. NGOs involved in TANs employ people who are professionally trained in the areas they address: in international law, development economics, health care management, the provision of essential services, and so on. TANs are most conspicuously *unlike* 'counterpublic spheres', then, precisely in that those involved tend *not* to be people who are directly affected by the issues. The people involved in negotiating with IGOs are of a similar profile to those who are employed by IGOs themselves. They are well educated, well paid, and fortunate, while those for whom they work are marginalized politically and economically, often living in terrible poverty, sometimes in desperate situations of violence and social collapse.

Indeed, it is partly on these grounds that NGOs have been criticized as undemocratic, as elitist, technocratic, and out of touch with the everyday lives of those they claim to represent (Chandhoke 2002; Tarrow 2001). TANs are not necessarily oriented towards enabling discussion and debate between 'all affected' by a particular issue. Sometimes there are good reasons for this. In cases of gross violations of human rights, for example, although uncovering the truth and dealing with the consequences of genocide may be an outcome of successful advocacy at IGO level, in advance of persuading leaders to acknowledge and address abuses, it may simply be too dangerous for citizens to debate the regime within which they must live. However, NGOs are also criticized as undemocratic in that ultimately they can only survive as long as they are financially viable. It is argued that at root they are oriented towards their supporters and funders, regardless of the best interests of those for whom they are supposed to exist (Huddock 1999; Bob 2005). Again, those who decide which NGO projects should receive funding are *not* those affected by the issues involved.

Such criticisms focus on the democratic legitimacy of TANs: NGOs are criticized as neither representative of nor accountable to those who are affected by the issues they address. In terms of Fraser's theorization of normative legitimacy, TANs certainly do not measure up, detached as they tend to be from grassroots contestations of ideas and interests by 'all affected'. But what difference does it make if we consider the other aspect of Fraser's theorization of the global public sphere, 'efficacy'? How do TANs measure up in terms of democratic theory if efficacy is given greater attention and value?

Fraser states very precisely what she means by 'efficacy' in her analysis of Habermas's democratic theory. It involves, firstly, 'translation', by which she means that 'the communicative power generated in civil society must be translated first into binding laws and then into administrative power'. And secondly, efficacy involves 'capacity', which means that 'the public power must be able to implement the discursively formed will to which it is responsible' (p. 31, this volume). In other words, efficacy includes both the responsiveness of the state (in the national case) and IGOs (where politics is multi-scalar) to demands 'from below', and also their institutional capacities to actually enact what has been decided on. It involves the porousness and responsiveness of political institutions to public will, and also their capacity to resist pressure (from corporations, for example) that would distort what should be a just outcome of deliberation within those institutions. Fraser's analysis of the meaning of 'efficacy' is admirably, and characteristically, clear as an exegesis of the terms in which Habermas theorizes the importance of the public sphere to democracy in *Between Facts and Norms*. It seems to me, however, that it misses a third dimension of efficacy, more implied perhaps than explicit in Fraser's theory of 'counterpublic spheres', but one that is nevertheless very significant to her understanding of their contribution to democracy. In my view, Fraser's original theorization of how second-wave feminism contributed to democracy was in part dependent on what we might think of as its *usefulness*, on the extent to which it was actually able to influence both public debate and public policy. It is second-wave feminism's value as *useful*, as actually effective (at least in some respects), that makes its contribution to democracy worth theorizing.

As I understand Fraser's argument in 'Rethinking the Public Sphere', as well as readings of second-wave feminism more generally, the political practices of the feminist movement contributed to democracy largely as a kind of side-effect of struggles for justice, redistribution, and recognition (see also Fraser 2008a). Feminists contributed to democracy by contesting assumptions and norms that contributed to women's subordination, by trying out alternatives in their own lives, and by actually changing the social conditions of women's lives through policy-making and legislation (with regard to pay, opportunities, freedom from violence, etc.). Creative forms of democratic participation were certainly invented by the early second-wave movement, to facilitate equality of voices at meetings, to prevent domination by movement leaders, and so on. And creative ways of life were fostered too, as experiments in co-operative work and family life. But these concerned participation *internally* within the feminist counterpublic sphere. Externally, in relation to the mainstream, feminists were concerned not with improving democracy, but with how women might win justice and become empowered. The expansion of the counterpublic involved persuading fellow-citizens to change their lives – especially women, many of whom became part of a discursive space in which the phrase 'I'm not a feminist but . . .' prefaced feminist arguments and conclusions. To a lesser extent, the expansion of the counterpublic also involved translating demands into policy. The question of the democratic legitimacy of the society as a whole was not one of the burning issues of second-wave feminists. It is not accidental, I think, that the issue of women's formal representation in political institutions was raised very late in the twentieth century across North America and most of Europe, a fact that is reflected in the way that Fraser herself added 'representation' to 'redistribution' and 'recognition' as a categorization of forms of justice only quite recently (Fraser 2008b; see also Phillips 1991).

In my view, it is because feminism was *useful*, because it was actually effective in expanding conversations about gender and justice and altering women's lives, that it was democratizing. It was not *because* it was legitimate or *because* 'translation' and 'capacity' enabled some demands to be at least partially met that feminism enhanced democracy. Feminism altered the conditions under which women participate in all aspects of social life, not just in terms of discussing gender, and not only those women (and small numbers of men) who identified as feminists. It is insofar as feminism was useful, insofar as it effectively challenged existing cultural norms and social structures and opened up women's participation (regardless of whether they identified as feminists or not) as more than mere appendages of men, that it was democratizing.

Opening up the concept of 'efficacy' to include 'usefulness' as well as 'translation' and 'capacity' gives us some insight, I think, into the contribution some NGOs are making to global democracy. TANs are concerned above all to be useful; they are not directly concerned with democratic legitimacy. To be sure, like social movements activists, individuals who work in TANs are likely to be motivated by feelings of indignation at their views being excluded from political life, at the national or the international level, and they are very likely to express the view that exclusion itself is illegitimate – whether it is seen as a consequence of the power of multinational corporations or of large and wealthy states like the US. But their concern is very rarely directed at improving the quality or the inclusivity of public debate as such, and nor does it necessarily do so. It is much more likely to be focused on a particular issue, place, or group of people and on what can practically be done to remedy injustice and ameliorate conditions that are causing suffering. It is generally only indirectly that TANs are concerned with making institutions of global governance more accountable to stakeholders. TANs aim to make a difference to international regulation that affects political, social, and economic conditions within and across states on behalf of those who are affected by global governance. If they are successful, they may increase the porousness of international political institutions to non-state actors, the possibility of 'translating' dissatisfaction with those institutions upwards, but generally this is a kind of side-effect of their practical aims to directly impact on regulation and policy decisions.

The paradigm case here is NGO work on securing human rights, which has been extensively researched by those who work on TANs. In the case of human rights violations, Keck and Sikkink argue that where lip service is paid to norms by international leaders, there is the possibility of moral leverage, allowing the gap between rhetoric and practice to be exposed, and opening up the possibility of real change in repressive or negligent states. There is a body of empirical evidence to support their argument, indicating that NGOs can successfully apply pressure through IGOs on state elites to change institutions in which murder, torture, and 'disappearance' are routine ways of dealing with political opposition (Hafner-Burton and Tsutusi 2005; Risse et al. 1999). In such cases, instead of ignoring or tolerating gross violations of human rights, officials working in IGOs take measures to shame those of their fellows who are complicit with such practices in their own states, whilst at the same time assisting them to build capacity – training security forces, monitoring elections, and so on. Of course, human rights have a special relationship to democracy. In complex societies in which state actors have access to means of surveillance and violence unprecedented in human history, popular participation in politics is impossible in any form without a framework that ensures respect for fundamental civil and political freedoms. My point here, however, is not to do with the usefulness of TANs in securing human rights as such as a condition of democratization. The more general point is that, on occasion, where TANS effectively bring institutions of global governance to account for failing to observe their own terms of association (whether that involves respecting human rights, keeping the peace, or enabling equitable development), they may also make them a little more responsive to people's needs (in the case of securing human rights, the need is for freedom to engage in politics). Where TANs alter the terms and conditions through which global governance is conducted in ways that make IGOs more accountable and therefore a little more responsive to people's needs, they make a small but significant contribution to postnational democratization even though they themselves are not democratically legitimate.

Conclusion

Given the ethos of critical theory as involving the elaboration of normative ideals in relation to ongoing political practice, it seems to me that Habermas's theory of the transnational public sphere 'scaled up' is too far from what is actually possible to be of much use to postnational democratization. I have addressed this problem by considering the two aspects of democracy that Fraser analyses in terms of Habermas's political theory of the public sphere: normative legitimacy, the claim that a transnational public sphere must enable democratic discussion between 'all affected' by a particular issue; and political efficacy, that a transnational public sphere must influence, or even form, accountable political institutions that act for 'all affected' through binding law and administration. I have raised the question of normative legitimacy in relation to Habermas's revised understanding of the public sphere at the national level, suggesting that the fundamental problem is less 'scaling up' than how the plural, 'subjectless' mediated public might work in practice even at the national level. In terms of efficacy, I have suggested that Fraser's theory of counterpublic spheres implies a third aspect of democratization, besides 'translation' and 'capacity', that I have called 'usefulness'. 'Usefulness' might be summarized as the ability to actually make a difference. In the sense in which I have discussed it here, it is not actually confined to dealings with the state. As I have argued, it should also be understood as necessary to democratization in terms of the concrete effectiveness of a movement, organization, or network in contesting hegemonic knowledge and assumptions in civil society. Without 'usefulness', counterpublic spheres do not contribute to democratization in civil society, however legitimate they may be. In terms of postnational democracy, however, what is equally if not more important now is 'usefulness' in opening up institutional possibilities for justice and empowerment of the most politically and economically marginalized. Institutions of global governance are even more distant from the concerns of most people than are those of national states, they are closed to those who do not speak the expert languages of science and law, and they are weak in that they are concerned at least as much with geopolitical rivalry as with making global policy for the good of all. In these circumstances, successfully contesting the closure of administrative thinking and procedures that do not take account of the people who suffer the consequences of the decisions made in global governance is an important contribution to postnational democracy. How useful TANs may actually be in any particular case, or indeed in general, is an empirical question. Critical assessment of their success in influencing IGOs in general is extremely complex (see the case studies in Scholte 2011). Perhaps the most serious limitation of these efforts is that TANs, concerned as they are with the technocratic adjustment of existing policies, do nothing to address the fundamental inequities between states which make them sites for geopolitical power play rather than principled policy-making. They do little in this respect to aid the 'capacity' of international political institutions in relation to the wealthiest and most powerful states, which is surely one of the most difficult, and contentious, issues of global democracy. What is important here in terms of normative political theory, however, is that even though both their usefulness and their legitimacy are undoubtedly limited, NGOs may nevertheless contribute to global democracy insofar as they alter the discursive and institutional conditions that make global justice and democracy impossible at the global scale. Paradoxically, in the current conditions of global governance, even undemocratic TANS may be democratizing if they make global governance a little more accountable and responsive to people's needs.

In conclusion, then, I have argued here that the terms of Fraser's analysis of feminism as a democratizing force, closely linked to actual political practice, is a better guide to what is possible today than the more abstract terms of Habermas's revised theory of the public sphere. Fraser's critical methodology is broadly similar to Habermas's in that, as I noted at the beginning of this essay, they share an interest in analysing emancipatory possibilities and normative ideals that are significant in reality, testing them in thought, and elaborating guidelines for political practice. It seems to me, however, that Fraser's approach is somewhat different in its starting point. What she does in her justly celebrated article on 'counterpublic spheres' is to take feminism as a kind of 'exemplary ideal' out of which to understand possibilities of democracy. If we are to understand possibilities of postnational democratization, it seems to me that we might also begin with 'actually existing' efforts to make global governance more open, responsive, and effective at addressing the issues and structures that affect the most impoverished and marginalized people in the world today.

References

Bob, C. (2005) *The Marketing of Rebellion: Insurgents, Media and International Activism.* Cambridge: Cambridge University Press.

Calhoun, C. (ed.) (1992) *Habermas and the Public Sphere.* Cambridge, MA: MIT Press.

Castells, M. (2009) *Communication Power.* Oxford: Oxford University Press.

Chandhoke, N. (2002) 'The Limits of Global Civil Society', in M. Glasius, M. Kaldor, and H. Anheier (eds), *Global Civil Society Yearbook 2002.* Oxford: Oxford University Press.

Fraser, N. (1997) 'Rethinking the Public Sphere: A Contribution to the Critique of Actually Existing Democracy', in *Justice Interruptus: Critical Reflections on the 'Postsocialist Condition'.* New York and London: Routledge.

Fraser, N. (2008a) 'Mapping the Feminist Imagination: From Redistribution to Recognition to Representation', in *Scales of Justice: Reimagining Political Space in a Globalizing World.* Cambridge: Polity.

Fraser, N. (2008b) 'The Politics of Framing: An Interview with Nancy Fraser [by Kate Nash and Vikki Bell]', in *Scales of Justice: Reimagining Political Space in a Globalizing World.* Cambridge: Polity.

Habermas, J. (1989) *The Structural Transformation of the Public Sphere*, trans. T. Burger. Cambridge: Polity.

Habermas, J. (1996) *Between Facts and Norms: Contributions to a Discourse Theory of Law and Democracy*, trans. W. Rehg. Cambridge: Polity.

Hafner-Burton, E. and K. Tsutusi (2005) 'Human Rights Practices in a Globalizing World: The Paradox of Empty Promises', *American Journal of Sociology* 110(5): 1373–411.

Huddock, A. (1999) *NGOs and Civil Society: Democracy by Proxy?* Oxford: Oxford University Press.

Keck, M.E. and K. Sikkink (1998a) *Activists beyond Borders: Advocacy Networks in International Politics.* Ithaca, NY: Cornell University Press.

Keck, M.E. and K. Sikkink (1998b) 'Transnational Advocacy Networks in the Movement Society', in D. Meyers and S. Tarrow (eds), *The Social Movement Society: Contentious Politics for a New Century.* Lanham, MD: Rowman and Littlefield.

Landes, J. (ed.) (1998) *Feminism, the Public and the Private.* Oxford: Oxford University Press.

Melucci, A. (1989) *Nomads of the Present: Social Movements and Individual Needs in Contemporary Society.* Philadelphia: Temple University Press.

Nash, K. (2009) *The Cultural Politics of Human Rights: Comparing the US and UK.* Cambridge: Cambridge University Press.

Norval, A. (2007) *Aversive Democracy: Inheritance and Originality in the Democratic Tradition.* Cambridge: Cambridge University Press.

Phillips, A. (1991) *Engendering Democracy.* Cambridge: Polity.

Risse, T.S. Ropp, and K. Sikkink (1999) *The Power of Human Rights: Institutional Norms and Domestic Change.* Cambridge: Cambridge University Press.

Scholte, J. (ed.) (2011) *Building Global Democracy? Civil Society and Accountable Global Governance.* Cambridge: Cambridge University Press.

Tarrow, S. (2001) 'Transnational Politics: Contention and Institutions in International Politics', *Annual Review of Political Science* 4: 1–20.

Tarrow, S. (2005) *The New Transnational Activism.* Cambridge: Cambridge University Press.

Thompson, J.B. (1995) *The Media and Modernity: A Social Theory of the Media.* Cambridge: Polity.

4

An Alternative Transnational Public Sphere?

On Anarchist Cosmopolitanism in Post-Westphalian Times

Fuyuki Kurasawa

In 'Transnationalizing the Public Sphere', Nancy Fraser performs a vital task for critical theory today, namely, the postnational reframing of one of the most influential concepts to have appeared in the human sciences over the last few decades. Since it was published in 1962, and belatedly appeared in an English-language translation in 1989, Habermas's *The Structural Transformation of the Public Sphere* (1989) has remained at the heart of intellectual debate and reflection in various parts of the world. Quite aside from the difficulties of updating a notion with such an intellectual pedigree and converting it in a transnational direction, Fraser is attempting to do so during a period of potential institutional transformation and transitional reorganization of social life (which the terms 'post-Westphalian' and 'postnational' are intended to capture). Unlike Habermas, whose retrospective narrative benefited from establishing a historical correspondence – and even an implicit relation of interdependence – between the formation of the public sphere and the parallel establishment of the nation-state form in Western

Europe, Fraser cannot draw upon equivalent or similarly thick institutional foundations to construct the normative and analytical foundations of a process of transnationalization of the public sphere. Accordingly, as she sees it, the latter's normativity precedes its actual institutionalization and should inform it, in order to embody and advance post-Westphalian principles of justice.

In the following pages, I want to interrogate Fraser's analysis of the transnationalization of the public sphere from the perspective of what could be termed an anarchist-inspired model of cosmopolitanism. Through this lens, the realization of global justice via a structural transformation of the world order in the direction of egalitarian universalism and participatory democracy can be achieved less by public opinion working through public authorities within formal institutions of global governance than by the concretization of counterpublicity in modes of democratic self-organizing and self-management within national and global civil societies.[1] I will proceed by revisiting and utilizing certain insights from Fraser's earlier (1992) reconceptualization of Habermasian public-sphere theory (Fraser 1992), which is summarized in 'Transnationalizing the Public Sphere' (pp. 16–17, this volume), but which raises questions germane to the project of reflecting on globally oriented emancipatory struggles in our age. Specifically, two of Fraser's key arguments, initially presented in that earlier piece, can fruitfully be linked to her post-Westphalian reimagining of justice and employed to support an anarchist-derived understanding of cosmopolitanism and global justice: her post-bourgeois conception of the public sphere, through which she argues that the latter may be understood as a sphere for both opinion formation and decision-making in democratic societies; and her well-known notion of subaltern counterpublics, which designate 'parallel discursive arenas where members of subordinated social groups invent and circulate counterdiscourses to formulate oppositional interpretations of their identities, interests, and needs' (Fraser 1992: 123).

Accordingly, this essay begins by homing in on a specific aspect of Fraser's post-bourgeois reframing of public-sphere theory, namely, her discussion of two kinds of strong decision-making publics: parliamentary institutions or public authorities blurring the line between civil society and the state (or institutions of global governance); and self-managed institutions within civil society (Fraser 1992: 134–5; pp. 16–17, this volume). The democratic responsiveness of the first type of strong public hinges upon the capacity of civil societies to hold it accountable, yet, at the same time, this public's blurring of the separation of civil society and the state (or institutions of global governance) may foster two tendencies that can themselves compromise such accountability: the subsumption and co-optation of public authorities within national and global infrastructures of governance; and the dilution of publicity's critical and oppositional function. However, as I will argue below, Fraser's ideas of 'self-managed institutions' as strong publics and of 'subaltern counterpublics' are much closer to the self-understandings and practices of many radical groups and activist movements within global civil society. Indeed, these groups and movements are often characterized by a strategy of 'engaged withdrawal' (Virno 1996) from the formal-institutional realm of national and global politics, yet use counterpublicity effectively to pursue a critique of the mainstream public sphere, the constitution of a transnational counterhegemonic bloc (or oppositional public spheres), and the multiplication of self-managed decision-making sites and projects across the world. Thus, would Fraser see a 'scaled-up' version of the idea of subaltern counterpublics as a productive lens through which to make sense of such political practices, and as a way to inform an anarchist cosmopolitanism supplementing her theory of the transnationalization of the public sphere?

Let us begin by turning to the first theme of this essay, the implications of some elements of Fraser's post-bourgeois reframing of the public sphere for the transnationalization of the public sphere.

Fuyuki Kurasawa

From a Post-Bourgeois to a Post-Westphalian Public Sphere

In 'Rethinking the Public Sphere' (1992), Fraser makes a compelling case for an understanding of the public sphere that goes beyond its liberal bourgeois iterations, which, by sharply distinguishing civil society[2] from the state, are self-limiting in restricting the role of the public sphere to that of weak publics concerned strictly with opinion formation (and not with decision-making, understood as the proper domain of the state).[3] For Fraser, Habermasian public-sphere theory has overlooked a significant, post-bourgeois development in democratic societies: that is to say, the emergence of parliamentary sovereignty and the consequent functioning of parliamentary institutions as a public sphere within the state. Parliaments function as strong publics involved in both public deliberation and decision-making, thus blurring the line dividing civil society from the state in a manner that she views as democratically beneficial, since public opinion is strengthened when an institution representing it can also convert it into authoritative decisions (Fraser 1992: 134–6).

When comparing this post-bourgeois framing of the public sphere with Fraser's subsequent post-Westphalian understanding of it, two types of arguments stand out for my purposes: those which are foregrounded in her earlier piece and can be applied explicitly in reimagining the transnational public sphere, and those which appear consistently in both texts and contain implications for the recasting of public sphere theory generally.

One of the key points emerging out of Fraser's post-bourgeois understanding of the public sphere consists of her distinction between two different instances of 'strong publics': aforementioned parliaments blurring the distinction of state and civil society, and self-managed institutions within civil society that could, she argues, constitute sites of direct or quasi-direct democracy whereby 'all those engaged in a collective undertaking would participate in deliberation to determine [the institution's] design and operation' (Fraser

1992: 135). The latter type of 'strong publics' opens up the prospect of a civil-society-centric model of the public sphere, in which self-managed groups are not restricted to public deliberation but engage in decision-making functions without necessary involvement with the state or equivalent governmental organizations in the formal-institutional track of democratic politics. However, aside from the mention of '"quasi-strong" decision-making publics in civil society' (p. 17, this volume) in her own overview of her earlier article, Fraser does not explore the implications of this idea of self-managed institutions as strong publics in 'Transnationalizing the Public Sphere'. She probably has three reasons for not doing so: the limited capacity of such 'narrower' strong publics to implement the collective will of national and global civil society; the question of accountability of these same publics to 'wider' publics at large, given that all those subjected or affected by the decisions of self-managed institutions are legitimately entitled to participate in their decision-making processes; and the complexity of inter-institutional co-ordination of self-managed groups or organizations.[4] Since Fraser's post-Westphalian analysis focuses upon the routing of public opinion through the formal-institutional domain – via public authorities or addressees operating like parliamentary institutions in a Westphalian setting – we can infer that she has in mind rather the former kind of 'strong publics' at this scale: those that blur the line separating institutions of governance from civil society because of their capacity to combine public deliberation and generalized decision-making at the transnational scale as well.

This formulation partially addresses the three concerns noted above. Nevertheless, the routing of publicity through formal-institutional politics introduces other problems from an anarchist perspective, in which the state and public authorities are viewed as structures monopolizing officially sanctioned modes of coercion and regulation of populations, as well as reproducing hierarchical relations between the governing and governed segments of these same populations.

Therefore, such public authorities or addressees, which exist outside of national and global civil societies, ought not to be delegated with the tasks of implementing the outcomes of deliberative processes taking place within these same civil societies. In other words, for anarchists, the externalization of legal and administrative capacities from civil society tends to reinforce the power that governmental institutions can exercise over persons and groups, a tendency that works against public opinion's ability to hold public authorities accountable owing to these governmental institutions' autopoietic dynamics (which will be explained below).

To my mind, the key to these potential limits is found in the reliance upon the capacity of public opinion within civil societies to hold public authorities accountable, in order to ensure that these decision-making strong publics located within national or transnational governmental institutions carry out the deliberative will of such civil societies. Public authorities' accountability to 'narrower' strong and weak publics within civil societies is essential if the former are to resist centripetal tendencies that would draw them 'inward' towards centres of decision-making power, whereby they would be entirely subsumed by and responsive to the imperatives of the formal-institutional domain of politics. And in a scenario of representative democracy in which public authorities are so significant as the executors of delib-erative consensus in civil society, the representative legiti-macy of their decisions hinges upon how closely such decisions correspond, and are accountable, to the will of the people (i.e., respecting the principle of popular sovereignty). Fraser is clearly concerned with the pivotal function of accountability in her framework, for her earlier piece asks '[w]hat institutional arrangements best ensure the account-ability of democratic decision-making bodies (strong publics) to *their* (external, weak, or, given the possibility of hybrid cases, weak*er*) publics?' (1992: 135, original emphasis). In 'Transnationalizing the Public Sphere', however, accounta-bility is linked explicitly only to political efficacy ('public opinion is considered efficacious if and only if it is mobilized as a political force to hold public power accountable' [p. 31, this volume]). Of course, it is implicitly linked to questions of the normative legitimacy of public opinion in relation to the inclusivity of participation in debate in the transnational public sphere. But Fraser does not specify in any detail mechanisms to enforce the accountability of public powers to civil societies, either in 'Rethinking' or in 'Transnational-izing',[5] something that is particularly significant given that these mechanisms must perform as countervailing forces against governing institutions' centripetal and colonizing effects upon such public powers. Even in a Westphalian context with a clearly defined national *demos* (anchored in national citizenship regimes) and media, public authorities and parliamentary institutions were only ever accountable to public opinion to a limited extent. Hence, in a globalizing setting, specifying stringent devices and effective political practices of accountability becomes an even more important task, for the *demos* to whom public powers are accountable and the geographical scope of the sovereignty of these public powers are both ambiguous and contested. Could the 'all-subjected principle' (Fraser 2008: 65–7), for instance, define who has a legitimate claim to participate in recalls of repre-sentatives, in national or transnational public authorities that do not reflect public opinion or are not willing to legally and administratively implement it? If so, what body would enforce recall measures, and how would accountability be assessed in light of substantively different public opinions amongst populations entitled to demand recalls? Would other stringent mechanisms of accountability be equally adapted to and effective in a post-Westphalian age, and if so, what would they be?

If the structural position of public authorities as strong decision-making publics blurring the divide between global civil society and governing institutions (states, international organizations, etc.) is necessary to ensure that public opinion is translated to the formal-institutional realm of politics and that such public opinion can be converted into legally binding and administratively visible outcomes, it may also imperil the independence of the transnational public sphere vis-à-vis the system of global governance. A major reason for this potential loss of the transnational public sphere's independence is the process of structural co-optation of the transnational public sphere by, or its subsumption within, the system of global governance in the formal-institutional track of democratic politics – something about which Habermas was acutely aware in his original, Westphalian formulation of the bourgeois public sphere (Habermas 1989; Fraser 1992: 134). In a post-Westphalian setting, this tendency unfolds when strong decision-making public authorities shift from being situated *within* formal institutions of global governance to being functionally *of* these same institutions, and thus wholly or partially disarticulated from the transnational public sphere. In other words, what risks occurring is a severing of the ties binding the two components of the transnational public sphere: namely, weak publics or strong self-managed institutions within national and global civil societies, on the one hand, and strong publics (i.e., public authorities) within the system of global governance, on the other. Consequently, both the capacity of global civil society to translate public opinion to governing institutions and its ability to hold public authorities accountable can be eroded, as these public authorities are pulled towards and absorbed by the autopoietic (Luhmann 1996) or self-referential process of the aforementioned system of global governance in which they are located. In this case, autopoiesis signifies that the formal-institutional logic of governing institutions (that of juridico-bureaucratic power) operates as a closed system increasingly immune to informal 'exogenous' inputs from global or national civil-society groups, and that such a system of governance is geared towards meeting its own 'endogenous' objectives – those of reproducing and furthering its capacity to exercise power through legal and administrative means. Hence, the principal source of accountability of representatives operating within public authorities can shift from their constituents (external weak publics within national and global civil societies) to the impersonal, juridico-bureaucratic requirements of the formal-institutional sphere of political life (the organizational functions of governance and rule). Simultaneously, what may unfold is a devaluing of the place of weak publics within the transnational public sphere, for deliberation and opinion formation can be instrumentally reduced by self-referential institutions of governance to the status of means to let global civil-society groups express themselves without having any impact upon official decision-making or, yet again, means to legitimize executive, legal, and administrative outcomes by appearing to consult and be accountable to public opinion. Put simply, the autopoietic and centripetal dynamics of mechanisms of global governance can convert the principle of sovereignty of public authorities (i.e., their decision-making capacity as strong publics) from a source of democratic representativeness and accountability to an instrument by which these authorities rule over civil societies through juridical and bureaucratic techniques. This possibility may be even more pronounced at the transnational scale, in light of the absence of direct or 'organic' fit between public authorities and nationally bounded (or otherwise defined) civil-society constituencies to hold the former accountable.

What are the effects of this potential loss of the transnational public sphere's autonomy as a source of exogenous critique of official institutions of governance? Firstly, it facilitates a structural tendency whereby public authorities, which are situated within such governing institutions, marginalize or dilute the most radical claims emerging from global and national civil-society groups (e.g., for the elimination of global capitalism or the questioning of these public authorities' democratic legitimacy to make decisions on behalf of populations). Since many of these groups with an anarchist bent are contesting the participation of strong publics within formal-institutional politics, their demands for political self-management and direct democracy, as well as the transcendence of a capitalist economic order, are unlikely to be accommodated by these very same strong publics – which, in essence, would have to consent to their own abolition or, at the very least, the erosion of their decision-making legitimacy. In other words, given their structural location within the formal-institutional realm of politics, public powers cannot advance or legally and administratively implement counterdiscourses from self-managed publics in civil society that put into question the very existence of such formal institutions of governance. Instead, these public authorities are more likely to selectively filter public opinion translated from national and global civil societies, thus being responsive to 'reasonable' claims for modest changes to the existing system of global governance while deeming counterpublicity rejecting the democratic legitimacy of representative institutions within the formal-institutional sphere to be 'unreasonable', 'unrealistic', or 'irresponsible'. Therefore, the interpenetration of governing institutions and civil society via governing institutions enables the latter to absorb and tame demands for the radical reorganization of the global order, leading to reforms that appear to be accountable to segments of public opinion putting forth such demands while ensuring the reproduction of the structural foundations of this global order. One can think, for instance, of how the critical voices of certain progressive development nongovernmental organizations have been neutralized over time, as they have been gradually incorporated into and become participants in 'mainstream' exercises in global economic governance led by international financial institutions (the International Monetary Fund and the World Bank), which have been able to claim widespread civil-society consultation in decision-making without substantially modifying their neoliberal policies (Cooke 2003; Rückert 2007).

A second problem of the post-bourgeois model of 'strong publics', at national and transnational scales, originates from the increased vulnerability of civil-society-based practices of resistance to governmental regulation. As strong publics within governmental institutions, public authorities may serve not only to translate public opinion 'upwards' from civil society to these governmental institutions, but also to facilitate the penetration of technologies of governance 'downwards' from such institutions to national and global civil societies. Public powers, then, can serve as vehicles for the deployment of legal and administrative apparatuses to regulate civil-society groups, whether this is expressed in Habermas's diagnosis of the colonization of the lifeworld by the system (Habermas 1987) or Foucault's notion of the exercise of governmental power through the policing of populations and their modes of conduct (Foucault 1982). Governmental regulation is of particular concern for activist movements in global civil society, whose modes of direct action against global injustices can be impeded because enframed by juridical rules and administrative oversight. Public authorities may employ the rule of law and bureaucratic mechanisms to oversee the activities of persons and groups engaging in public acts of dissent and resistance, notably by officially sanctioning certain forms of political action and discourse as legitimate and condemning others as illegitimate. The latter category, applied to most acts of civil disobedience and deliberate violation of established legal and administrative statutes pursued by radical civil-society groups today (assistance to undocumented migrants, blockades against the occupation of indigenous land, sabotage of the material or virtual assets of transnational corporations, etc.), legitimizes numerous forms of governmental control: the passing of stricter border control legislation and deportation procedures, and the denial of migrant populations' civil and political rights, by parliamentary institutions in response to public campaigns by radical migration justice activists, or the legislative bolstering of international copyright regimes to facilitate the prosecution of anti-copyright campaigners because of their demands for fair use and free public distribution of cultural and intellectual goods.

Obviously, both the subsumption of the transnational public sphere within the system of global governance and the co-optation of exogenous critique are contrary to Fraser's intentions in devising her post-Westphalian model of 'reflexive justice' in which contestation plays a pivotal role (Fraser, chapter 1, this volume, and 2008). In addition they represent only potential consequences of the blurring of the separation of civil societies from governing institutions stemming from the structural position of public authorities within these governing institutions. Nevertheless, the point remains that such blurring can make public powers serve a variety of purposes: 'upwards' implementation of the collective will of civil society through legal and administrative outcomes, but, conversely, 'downwards' transmission of governmental regulation into national and global civil societies.

By contrast, Fraser's understanding of self-managed groups as 'strong publics' represents a fruitful undergirding for anarchist cosmopolitanism. For instance, one could imagine a transnational public sphere as a set of networks of self-managed councils and egalitarian spaces anchored through co-ordinating bodies at various geographical scales, practising forms of direct or quasi-direct democracy. Such networks would concretize two anarchist principles that insist on a suspicion of formal institutional reforms or juridico-administrative responses: collective autonomy, to ensure social self-instituting (the creation of laws and norms by people themselves); and direct action, types of interventions by civil-society groups against institutions that perpetrate global injustices (through acts of civil disobedience, disruptions of the functioning of transnational corporations and international financial institutions, the pursuit of experimental collectives, etc.). Like Fraser's post-bourgeois revision of the public sphere, this alternative model rejects the strict separation of civil society from the state, yet does so from the direction of recuperating or conserving within national and global civil societies the executive, legislative, and administrative functions conventionally attributed to governmental institutions; hence, all decision-making power would be preserved within civil society, where all strong and quasi-strong publics would reside, thereby enframing the formal-institutional realm of democratic politics. While such a model is not a panacea for the structural transformation of the world order, it does point to certain potential limits with a framework in which public powers and formal

institutions of national and global governance play promi-
nent roles in the realization of the will of civil society.

Global Civil-Society Activism as Subaltern Counterpublics

In addition to the idea of 'strong publics', in 'Rethinking the
Public Sphere' Fraser introduced the influential concept of
'subaltern counterpublics', which she defined as 'parallel discursive arenas where members of subordinated social groups
invent and circulate counterdiscourses to formulate oppositional interpretations of their identities, interests, and needs'
(1992: 123). Given the relatively minor place that the notion
occupies in 'Transnationalizing the Public Sphere', I would
be interested to know in much greater detail how Fraser
envisages the functioning and role of subaltern counterpublics within her post-Westphalian revision of public-sphere
theory. This strikes me as an important question given
the extent to which the idea of subaltern counterpublics
captures the informal, nongovernmental strategies and self-
understandings of many activist segments of global civil
society, notably within the World Social Forum (WSF) and
transnational anti-capitalist struggles (Hardt 2002; Notes
from Nowhere 2003; Sen and Waterman 2009).[6] Specifically,
in her earlier piece, Fraser (1992: 124) describes the 'dual
orientation' of subaltern counterpublics in a manner that
sheds light on these segments' modes of political practice. At
one level, several radical groups within global civil society
are committed to tactics of 'withdrawal and regroupment'
or 'engaged withdrawal' (Virno 1996) from both 'mainstream' publics and the formal-institutional sphere of
democratic politics, in order to perform two types of 'under-
ground' political projects: direct action against organizations perpetuating structural inequalities and global injustices
(international financial institutions, transnational corporations, etc.); and the establishment of self-managed sites and
institutions performing as strong or quasi-strong publics in
civil society, which generate counterpublicity and whose

participants collectively determine how to organize their socio-political lives. At another level, these groups are equally committed to publicity via the dissemination of critical discourses and the pursuit of 'agitational activities' (Fraser 1992: 124) directed at wider publics within global and national civil societies, as well as the creation of oppositional public spheres or counterhegemonic blocs in which to deliberate about and denounce global injustices. In pursuing either of these functions (engaged withdrawal or publicity), then, progressive activist segments of global civil society are clearly not concentrating on influencing public powers within structures of global governance, and may in fact favour a transnational public sphere that rejects engagement with the formal-institutional domain of democratic politics.

Instead of such engagement, activist coalitions such as the WSF are attempting to devise an oppositional public sphere or counterhegemonic bloc composed of self-managed institutions within civil society, whose strategy of 'dodging' public authorities and formal-institutional arenas of politics more generally is grounded in the problematizing of three principles: the delegation of general decision-making, legal, and administrative power to public authorities, which activist coalitions view as leading to heteronomy (opposed to principles of collective autonomy via self-management); the capacity of public authorities to act as representatives of public opinion and defenders of the public interest (opposed to ideas about political self-reliance and direct action by subordinate and historically marginalized groups to defend their interests); and the imbrication of these public authorities within national or transnational systems of governance (opposed to an understanding of an independent transnational public sphere, or an oppositional public sphere outside of the latter and of these systems of governance).

Yet how are we to assess the extent to which these sorts of public discourses and strategies by subaltern counterpublics are politically impactful? For Fraser, following public-sphere theory, '[P]ublic opinion is considered efficacious if and only if it is mobilized as a political force to hold public power accountable, ensuring that the latter's exercise reflects the considered will of civil society' (p. 31, this volume).[7] However, would she consider expanding the understanding of public opinion's political efficacy to account for informal, non-institutional, and even anti-institutional forms of publicity by subaltern counterpublics (e.g., those found in the WSF), which neither are directed towards influencing public powers nor depend upon implementation of decisions by these public powers in order to yield structural transformations of the current world order?[8] Let me suggest three criteria that, by supplementing the notion of capacity to hold public authorities accountable, could help gauge counterpublicity's political efficacy: firstly, the fostering of agonistic contest in global civil society, to put into question self-evident, mainstream public opinion consensus about the established world order (e.g., Gramscian hegemonic worldviews or Bourdieusian doxa about the absence of alternatives to neoliberal capitalism); secondly, the enabling of egalitarian practices of direct or quasi-direct democracy, which resist the delegation of executive, legal, and administrative power to a sphere of formal-institutional politics; and, thirdly, the cultivation of autonomy via self-managed councils and collectives, as well as of alternative projects of organization of social life built on principles of solidaristic mutual aid, participatory democracy, and egalitarian universalism.

If assessed on the basis of these criteria, forms of counterpublicity that follow strategies of engaged withdrawal from official politics may be more effective than those routing their demands via public authorities. Such modes of counterpublicity, practised by subaltern counterpublics, can foster greater contestation of the hierarchical division between governing and governed subjects. At the same time, however, the political effectivity of these forms of counterpublicity in implementing progressive social change may be enhanced by dodging governmental regulation and averting institutional co-optation, thereby remaining uncompromising, oppositional critics of dominant public opinion as well as unpredictable, disruptive forces that draw upon their capacity to rapidly assemble, disperse, and eventually reappear in a different form to perform subversive, emancipatory acts.[9]

Conclusion

I have argued here that thinking about the transnationalization of the public sphere might usefully draw on concepts from Fraser's earlier work on the post-bourgeois public sphere. On the one hand, it is unclear whether there is a place for self-managed institutions as strong publics at the transnational scale, and if so, what she sees as their role in a post-Westphalian context. On the other, her idea of subaltern counterpublics remains useful to make sense of an oppositional strategy of engaged withdrawal from formal-institutional politics within significant segments of global civil-society activism today. To be sure, this argument only begins to touch upon three conventional weaknesses of anarchism as a tradition of thought, which will eventually need to be addressed if we are to formulate a compelling model of anarchist cosmopolitanism. Firstly, this model will need to envisage mechanisms of inter-organizational co-ordination amongst strong publics in global civil society that compose counterhegemonic transnational networks, in order to propose means of arriving at a generalized decisional consensus amongst self-managed institutions and activist groups. Secondly, an anarchist framework concerned with global justice should deal with the question of how to ensure the democratic accountability of subaltern counterpublics to wider publics within the transnational public sphere (Fraser 1992: 135), as well as how they can be participatively inclusive of all those subjected to the effects of their decisions (Fraser 2008). And thirdly, such a paradigm must specify the relation between the two tracks of the dialogical process in democratic politics, namely, the civil-society track embodied by the autonomous strategies that many transnational activist movements and coalitions pursue (upon which anarchism has concentrated) and the formal-institutional track of official global governance (which has been neglected by anarchist thinking). Nonetheless, to my mind, this kind of anarchist cosmopolitanism, embodied as it is in radical movements and groups in global civil society, raises important issues for Fraser's post-Westphalian revisioning of public-sphere theory. It offers a different position from which to consider the structural location of decision-making publics within the transnational public sphere and the political impact of counterpublicity emanating from informal, anti-governmental modes of transnational political activism performed by subaltern counterpublics. Conversely, it would be interesting to know how Fraser views the application of a 'scaled-up' version of her concept of subaltern counterpublics to inform anarchist cosmopolitanism, both to interpret practices of political struggle for global justice and to complement her theory of the transnationalizing public sphere.

Notes

Research and writing of this essay was made possible by a Standard Research Grant from the Social Sciences and Humanities Research Council of Canada. I would like to thank Kate Nash for her comments and wise editorial guidance.

1 I follow Negt and Klüge (1993) in understanding counterpublicity as forms of public opinion generated in an oppositional or proletarian public sphere, as a critique of the mainstream or bourgeois public sphere. As for civil society, I follow Fraser's definition (see following note).
2 Fraser uses an understanding of civil society as 'the nexus of nongovernmental or "secondary" associations that are neither economic nor administrative' (1992: 133).
3 Fraser defines weak publics as 'publics whose deliberative practice consists exclusively in opinion formation and does not also encompass decision making' (1992: 134) or those that 'generate public opinion but not binding laws' (p. 16, this volume), and strong publics as 'publics whose discourse encompasses both opinion formation and decision making' (1992: 134) or '"strong publics" within the state, whose deliberations issue in sovereign decisions' (p. 16, this volume).

4 The problems are already raised in Fraser's earlier article (Fraser 1992: 135–6) and only become amplified in a post-Westphalian setting in which neither accountability nor legitimacy of public opinion is restricted by geographical territory or political citizenship.

5 In an endnote to 'Rethinking the Public Sphere', Fraser does mention 'hybrid possibilities', 'arrangements involving very strict accountability of representative decision-making bodies to their external publics through veto and recall rights', adding that '[s]uch hybrid forms might be desirable in some circumstances, though certainly not all' (1992: 142 n. 37)

6 As Feher puts it, '[A]ctivists who follow the second path look for ways to eschew the prescriptions to which they object and, by doing so, secure a social space where the targets of these prescriptions can develop alternative ways of governing themselves and of relating to each other' (2007: 17).

7 In addition, Fraser specifies that publicity's political efficacy requires two conditions: a translation condition, whereby 'communicative power generated in civil society must be translated first into binding laws and then into administrative power'; and a capacity condition, whereby 'the public power must be able to implement the discursively formed will to which it is responsible' (p. 31, this volume).

8 Habermas has gone some way in revising his theory of the public sphere to recognize more explicitly the political efficacy of informal practices and discourses by civil-society actors (1996: 380–1).

9 For instance, activist groups rely on their informal character (i.e., their absence of official leaders, set tactics, or fixed organizational structures) to complicate and subvert the policing of alternative globalization and anti-G20 or anti-G8 protests (Notes from Nowhere 2003).

References

Cooke, B. (2003) 'A New Continuity with Colonial Administration: Participation in Development Management', *Third World Quarterly* 24(1): 47–61.

Feher, M. (2007) 'The Governed in Politics', in M. Feher (ed.), *Nongovernmental Politics*. New York: Zone Books.

Foucault, M. (1982) 'The Subject and Power', *Critical Inquiry* 8(4); 777–95.

Fraser, N. (1992). 'Rethinking the Public Sphere: A Contribution to the Critique of Actually Existing Democracy', in C. Calhoun (ed.), *Habermas and the Public Sphere*. Cambridge, MA: MIT Press.

Fraser, N. (2008) 'Abnormal Justice', in *Scales of Justice: Reimagining Political Space in a Globalizing World*. Cambridge: Polity.

Habermas, J. (1987) *The Theory of Communicative Action, Vol. 2: Lifeworld and System: A Critique of Functionalist Reason*, trans. T. McCarthy. Boston: Beacon Press.

Habermas, J. (1989) *The Structural Transformation of the Public Sphere: An Inquiry into a Category of Bourgeois Society*, trans. T. Burger with F. Lawrence. Cambridge: Polity.

Habermas, J. (1996) *Between Facts and Norms: Contributions to a Discourse Theory of Law and Democracy*, trans. W. Rehg. Cambridge: Polity.

Hardt, M. (2002) 'Today's Bandung?', *New Left Review* 14(Mar.–Apr.): 112–18.

Luhmann, N. (1996) *Social Systems*, trans. D. Baecker and J. Bednarz. Stanford: Stanford University Press.

Negt, O. and A. Klüge (1993). *Public Sphere and Experience: Toward an Analysis of the Bourgeois and Proletarian Public Sphere*, trans. P. Labanyi, J.O. Daniel, and A. Oksiloff. Minneapolis: University of Minnesota Press.

Notes from Nowhere (ed.) (2003). *We Are Everywhere: The Irresistible Rise of Global Anticapitalism*. London and New York: Verso.

Rückert, A. (2007) 'Producing Neoliberal Hegemony? A Neo-Gramscian Analysis of the Poverty Reduction Strategy Paper (PRSP) in Nicaragua', *Studies in Political Economy* 79: 91–118.

Sen, J. and P. Waterman (eds) (2009) *World Social Forum: Challenging Empires*. Montreal: Black Rose.

Virno, P. (1996) 'Virtuosity and Revolution: The Political Theory of Exodus', in P. Virno and M. Hardt (eds), *Radical Thought in Italy: A Potential Politics*. Minneapolis: University of Minnesota Press.

5

Time, Politics, and Critique
Rethinking the 'When' Question

Kimberly Hutchings

History and Critique

Over the last several years, Nancy Fraser has joined a chorus of normative theorists of justice and democracy who claim that theories of justice and democracy need to be rethought in the light of significant changes in the historical context in which those theories are formulated. In Fraser's case, this claim is made by a theorist working in a Frankfurt School tradition of critical theory in which critique is grounded in a thorough appreciation of the emancipatory potential peculiar to any given historical 'constellation'. In an interview published in *Signs*, Fraser refers to her view that we are currently in an era in which an epochal shift is taking place: 'Call it globalization for want of a better term' (Fraser and Naples 2004: 1108). In discussing globalization, Fraser emphasizes both its novelty and the extent to which it undermines the territorial state as the political frame for addressing questions of justice and democracy. Globalization is about 'a new sense of vulnerability to transnational forces' that effectively disrupts previously accepted constraints on answers to the 'who', 'how', 'what', and 'where' of both justice and democracy. According to Fraser, answers to these questions used to be stabilized by the 'Westphalian' order of the modern liberal capitalist state, but those answers are no longer satisfactory given the historical shift to a 'post-Westphalian' frame. This has a whole range of implications for the principles of social justice (distributive and recognitive) for which Fraser has argued in the past, and for her commitment to radically democratic politics within both formal (state) and informal (civil society) spheres.

Fraser's argument about the need to rethink the public sphere (again) is one aspect of her broader project – that of reframing principles of justice and democracy in a post-Westphalian era. As she points out, from her own critical-theoretical point of view, Habermas's original formulation of the role of the public sphere was flawed in a variety of respects. In particular, it presumed too much in terms of the actual accessibility and equality of processes of opinion formation characteristic of the public sphere within the liberal state. This resulted in accounts of the public sphere that effectively occluded inequalities of power and patterns of exclusion characteristic of Western liberal democracies, and undermined the critical potential of the public sphere in practice. In her earlier reformulation of Habermas's ideas, Fraser (1992) argued both for a pluralization of the critical conceptualization of the public sphere, to include subaltern publics and counterpublics, and for a better understanding of the conditions through which a variety of publics could flourish, in terms of legitimacy and efficacy. On her account, the public sphere remained crucial to an ideal of democracy as a context within which the views of different publics could be discursively formulated, and thereby as an arena for the articulation of new claims to justice. The public sphere, as both a particular discursive ideal and an empirical reality, was a central location for the critique and renewal of democratic politics.

In Fraser's view, the conservativism in accounts of the public sphere in the liberal state, of which she was critical in her early work, is in danger of being carried over into contemporary arguments concerning transnational public spheres. Contemporary interest in transnational publics, she suggests, does not look seriously enough at the principles that need to underlie transnational public spheres if they are to serve any kind of critical function within a globalizing world. If the critical potential of the public sphere is to be rescued, then its conceptualization within critical theory needs to be revisited and reworked in the light of both the principles of communicative reason and contemporary post-Westphalian historical conditions.

Fraser is explicit about the fact that her argument concerning the need to revisit the critical potential of the idea of the public sphere depends on her reading of the present as involving the 'structural transformation' of public spheres and their conditions of possibility. This structural transformation follows from a whole set of developments associated with neoliberal globalization, in which processes of communication, political issues, the 'publics' affected by political policies and decisions, and the actors making policy and taking decisions have all become transnationalized. On Fraser's account, Habermasian theories of the public sphere gained their plausibility, in part, from the Westphalian frame of reference in which they were embedded. She argues that the critical purchase of these theories relied on their ability to make a case for the legitimacy and efficacy of public opinion. This, in turn, rested on the capacity of these theories to offer a sustainable account of the 'who' and 'how' of public opinion formation and expression, and of the processes through which public opinion could gain efficacious purchase on the addressee of its claims and arguments. Fraser argues that although the 'how' of public opinion was open to contestation and debate within theories of the public sphere, the 'who' was simply taken for granted as equivalent to the citizenry of the Westphalian nation-state. Similarly, the translation and capacity conditions for the efficacy of the public sphere were bound up with the assumption of the state as the relevant public power, capable both of legislating and implementing the public's demands. In other words, in particular in relation to 'who' and to capacity conditions, the nation-state provided a kind of short-cut for the specification of how a genuinely critical public sphere might work. According to Fraser, this short-cut is no longer possible because of a historical shift to a post-Westphalian frame, in which neither communicative publics nor systemic powers correlate to the sovereign power of the Westphalian nation-state.

> The 'who' of communication, previously theorized as a Westphalian-national citizenry, is often now a collection of dispersed interlocutors, who do not constitute a *demos*. The 'what' of communication, previously theorized as a Westphalian-national interest rooted in Westphalian-national economy, now stretches across vast reaches of the globe, in a transnational community of risk, which is not, however, reflected in concomitantly expansive solidarities and identities. The 'where' of communication, once theorized as the Westphalian-national territory, is now deterritorialized cyberspace. The 'how' of communication, once theorized as Westphalian-national print media, now encompasses a vast translinguistic nexus of disjoint and overlapping visual cultures. (p. 26, this volume)

The above quotation presents a 'before and after' story, in which theoretical accounts of the public sphere are argued to have become outdated insofar as they no longer correspond to the realities of the present. For Fraser, a critical theory of the public sphere can only become meaningful again to the extent that it treats these new circumstances as its point of departure. This is crucial because the critical power of any such reformulated theory of the public sphere must derive from the normative resources immanent in historical development, as opposed to a set of ahistorical moral principles. For Fraser, globalization amounts to an epochal change because it has cut across state boundaries and undermined state autonomy from both above and below. This account presumes a Westphalian sovereignty phase as norm, which is then undermined by globalization. On reflection, however, this does not correspond to the experience of most states, civil societies, or public spheres. For most states, for example, global neoliberalism is simply the latest in a long line of ways in which domestic policy is externally constrained, and in most civil societies and public spheres, the terms of debate about justice and democracy have always crossed the boundaries of political community and often been set elsewhere. To the extent that the Westphalian myth has ever applied in the way suggested in Fraser's historical analysis, it has been closest to the experience of what used to be called the 'first world', imperial and post-imperial states. Of course, this does not mean that Fraser's historical diagnosis is straightforwardly inaccurate, but it does suggest that her account of the current 'postnational constellation' is a partial one. This is evident in her own simultaneous acknowledgement and dismissal of the fact that political citizenship has not traditionally operated as a plausible proxy for the 'all-affected' principle for peoples outside of the perspective of the 'metropole' (p. 19, this volume).

But even if Fraser's account of the history through which we have arrived at this moment of postnational politics is partial, does this matter for her critical reformulation of the theory of the public sphere? Two arguments can be made to the effect that this doesn't really matter. According to the first argument, the fact that there are different histories of different public spheres is not important in comparison to the rational defensibility of the principles through which public spheres can be identified as a resource for the legitimate critique of power. This kind of argument is common in more abstract deontological versions of cosmopolitan justice and democracy, and it rests on the claim that the moral validity of claims can be detached from the historical context in which they arise. However, this kind of claim doesn't fit with the critical, historical approach we find in Fraser's work. For a critical theorist, it is the normative potential of the present that matters, and this cannot be identified by reference to ahistorical principles.

From Fraser's point of view, therefore, there must be an alternative response as to why the partial and 'Westphalian-centric' nature of her reading of history does not matter. The obvious response, suggested in Fraser's own rather rapid dismissal of other histories, is the argument that what matters is the present rather than the past, and the present of the public sphere *now* consists in 'dispersed interlocutors', 'a transnational community of risk', 'deterritorialized cyber-space' and 'a vast translinguistic nexus'. To the extent that in the contemporary world economic, social, political, and communicative relations are extensively globalized, then it doesn't matter for the critical potential of public spheres in this globalized world that different individuals, civil societies, and states may have arrived there via very different historical experiences and with very different collective memories. In this respect, the *when* of globalization, its universal *presentness*, becomes the key to reconstructing the 'who', 'how', 'what', and 'where' questions about the public sphere that used to be answered by the nation-state. The question this raises, however, is whether it is possible to theorize the *presentness* of the *present* in detachment from the unifying narrative of the past against which an understanding of the present has been articulated. And if there is no such unifying narrative, then what are the implications for the meaning of the *presentness* of the *present*?

Thinking the Present

I will go on to suggest that Fraser is able to envisage moving from the Westphalian to the post-Westphalian 'who', 'what', 'where', and 'how' of a new critical theory of the public sphere because she treats its constitution in terms that take for granted the temporal positioning of the Westphalian, statist account of the public sphere that she aims to transcend. In order to do this, I will focus on the two aspects of the critical potential of public spheres as Fraser identifies them: firstly, the potential for fellow members of the public sphere to communicate as peers; secondly, the link between transnational public spheres and the creation of new authorities that will enable the effective translation of their communicative power into action. I will focus in particular on the question of what 'peer' means between political actors who do not share the vision of the world as novel, in which Fraser's new 'who' is embedded. And I will also focus on the question of what the creation of new mechanisms of translation and capacity will mean to those who do not have confidence in the old ones on which to base their aspirations.

At the beginning of her argument, Fraser sets out the assumptions built into Habermas's original formulation of the idea of the public sphere; she then goes on to show how each assumption has been challenged by processes of globalization. In doing this, she reminds us of an important feature of Habermasian critical theory, which is that it is bound up with a particular account of the historical development of modernity. On this account, modernity is effectively the outcome of the 'twinning' of the distinctive logics of strategic and communicative reason: on the one hand, modernity is the functional response to increasing complexity; on the other hand, it is the flowering, at a phylogenetic level, of the presuppositions of communicative reason in universal ideals of individual freedom and equality. The task of critical theory is to tap into the ideals of freedom and equality inherent in modernity as a counter to the systemic forces also inherent in it. Principles of universal human rights and democratic legitimation embedded in the constitutions of liberal states are one of the ways in which communicative reason counters the effects of strategic rationality. The public sphere, embedded in vibrant civil society activity, operates in a similar manner. But it is only able to do so because it takes the distinctively modern form that Habermas traces as emerging initially in the bourgeois public sphere of late eighteenth-century Europe. At the end of Fraser's account of the assumptions built into Habermas's account of the public sphere, she summarizes the final assumption thus:

> . . . *Structural Transformation* traced the cultural origins of the public sphere to the letters and novels of eighteenth- and nineteenth-century print capitalism. It credited those bourgeois genres with creating a new subjective stance, through

which private individuals envisioned themselves as members of a public. . . . Thus, Habermas grounded the structure of public-sphere subjectivity in the very same vernacular literary forms that also gave rise to the imagined community of the nation. (p. 12, this volume)

In her critique of the Westphalian framing of the above aspect of Habermas's theoretical presuppositions in his account of the public sphere, Fraser runs together two conditions for the emergence of the public sphere: the first is the 'subjective stance, through which private individuals envisioned themselves as members of a public'; the second is the 'imagined community of the nation'. She quite rightly points out that the assumption of a national vernacular literature would be counterfactual in today's conditions, in which not only is there a growth in the hybridization of literary production and reception, but also the significance of literature has been largely displaced by other forms of cultural production. For this reason, she argues that it is no longer possible to make a connection between a national culture and the conditions of possibility of a public sphere: 'insofar as public spheres require the cultural support of shared social imaginaries, rooted in national literary cultures, it is hard to see them functioning effectively today' (p. 26, this volume). In drawing this conclusion, however, Fraser glosses over the distinctiveness of the 'subjective stance' nourished by bourgeois literary forms and its role in the 'shared social imaginary' of citizenship. The importance of bourgeois literary forms, on Habermas's account, did not lie solely in the ways in which they were written in the language shared by citizens who could identify themselves with a specific political membership. It also lay in the specifically modern notion of bourgeois subjectivity with which they were imbued, regardless of the language in which they were written. On Habermas's account, this literature both reflected and reinforced the self-reflexive mode of subjectivity which is historically produced by capitalism and the modern state, and which simultaneously opens up the entry of communicative rationality into social, economic, and political life. From this point of view, modern subjectivity is far more crucial to the formation of the public sphere than national identity, because it is only modern subjects who interpret member-ship of common political community in terms of equality and freedom, and only modern subjects who have the capac-ity to identify the distinctiveness of the *present* as modern (Habermas, 1989: 51–6).

Fraser's critique of Habermas points to the way in which a particular location for a shared social imaginary, that of the nation, is losing its salience, but does not question the appropriateness of his conception of the social imaginary of the modern subject. Neither does she address the question of whether we can assume the standpoint of the modern subject in putative members of transnational public spheres that are not the product of the time and space of the modern liberal state: '[W]hat turns a collection of people into fellow members of a public is not shared citizenship, but their co-imbrication in a common set of structures and/or institu-tions that affect their lives' (p. 30, this volume).

On Fraser's account, the work done by both national identity and bourgeois subjectivity in the origins of the public sphere should, in contemporary circumstances, be substi-tuted for by the 'all-affected' principle. As with many cosmopolitan theorists, she argues that the *fact* of the trans-national interconnection between, in the expression of David Held and Anthony McGrew, 'overlapping communities of fate' is in itself insufficient to constitute a transnational public (Held and McGrew 2001: 327). But how is the all-affected principle able to do this work? The fact of the global effects of modern states and capitalist markets is of long standing. As Fraser herself points out, the *demos* and mem-bership of the public sphere never actually coincided with those affected by the structures and institutions of states and capital (p. 29, this volume). This fact is only able to do the work that Fraser wants it to do because it is accompanied by assumptions that position members of these new publics as self-reflexive subjects who share, or potentially share, a social imaginary in which the relation to the *present* takes on a particular resonance. What links members of these publics together is a common understanding of the post-Westphalian nature of their fate, and the self-conscious apprehension that this is the meaning of the *present*. In keeping with the tradition of Habermasian critical theory, the critical resources on which the public sphere draws must be immanent in a particular stage of historical development, and must be recognized by political actors as immanent in that development. If the translation of the idea of the public sphere to the context of the transnational is to be possible, then the *present* must not only be the same, but also be recognized to be the same for the members of the public seeking to release the normative potential of the era in which they find themselves. A shared social imaginary embedded in specific understandings of the relation between past, present, and future is crucial to the enabling conditions of any public sphere.

> Henceforth, public opinion is legitimate if and only if it results from a communicative process in which all potentially affected can participate as peers, *regardless of political citizenship*. Demanding as it is, this new, post-Westphalian understanding of legitimacy constitutes a genuinely critical standard for evaluating existing forms of publicity in the present era. (p. 31, this volume, original emphasis)

Within critical theories of transnational public spheres, dialogue and deliberation provide the legitimate means to mediate between different ways in which claims to justice are formulated by different constituencies in different parts of the world. But dialogue and deliberation can only do their work if 'all affected' are not simply the recipients of global effects, but also grasp those effects as in some sense part of a shared narrative. In generalizing the post-Westphalian as a common orientation for judgement for those imbricated in 'common sets of structures/institutions that affect their lives', Fraser does something akin to the conflation of the 'how' and 'who' that she perceives in earlier theorizations of the public sphere. The members of new transnational public spheres may be thought of as potential peers because they are all positioned within a story that reflects the experience of Western modernity in general, and the fate of liberal-capitalist welfare states in the latter part of the twentieth century in particular. But if this is not actually a common spatio-temporal orientation, then it is not clear what can do the work of enabling commonality and, potentially, parity in the formation of public opinion. Political imaginaries with a different temporality, in which post-Westphalian has a different meaning, will suggest a different orientation for judgement or may undermine the assumption of a unitary spatio-temporal orientation altogether. Without the assumption of a common spatio-temporal orientation for political judgement, could a transnational public sphere be possible at all?

From Legitimacy to Efficacy

I have suggested above that the assumption of the shared novelty of the global present does a lot of work in rendering plausible Fraser's account of what a post-Westphalian critical theorization of the 'who' as well as the 'how' of transnational public opinion formation needs to encompass. In addition to this, however, Fraser is also concerned with the condition of political efficacy of the post-Westphalian public sphere, and the contemporary inadequacy of Westphalian answers to questions about how public opinion is effectively translated into policy. She points to the way in which the sovereign territorial state was traditionally both the addressee of public opinion and the source of the capacity to implement its demands. What has changed, she argues, is the capacity of states in the context of globalization to control large swathes of policy that deeply affect the needs and interests of their populations. In this respect, however democratic they may be, and however strong the relations of communication and accountability between civil society and state, no state any longer has the administrative capacity to solve the problems faced by its citizens: 'The challenge, accordingly, is twofold: on the one hand, to create new, transnational public powers; on the other, to make them accountable to new, transnational public spheres' (p. 33, this volume).

As with her account of the post-Westphalian 'who', Fraser's reading of post-Westphalian capacity conditions presumes a particular historical story. According to this story, there was a period when the state operated potentially as an appropriate locus for the translation and implementation of public opinion. This period has now passed, and it is necessary to think about new sorts of powers that might be able to relate in a more effective way to a new sort of public. I would argue, however, that Fraser's account of the need for a new set of critical aspirations for theories of the public sphere, to include the setting up of new administrative powers, demonstrates the reliance of her argument on a 'who' that occupies the same time and space of political agency. The possibility of the critical role of the public sphere in the Westphalian state emerged out of the interrelation between its 'legitimacy' and 'efficacy' conditions. What helped to ground the legitimacy of the public sphere within modern states, on the Habermasian account, was precisely the correlation between 'state' and 'people' inherent in modern ideals of popular self-determination. The possibility of different effects being experienced as in some sense common by successive generations of aspirants to inclusion within the public sphere of the modern state was conditioned by their capacity to identify themselves as members of a particular collective history, a shared past, present, and future. In turn, this identification was conditioned by the experienced effectiveness of state power in relation to both internal and external populations, and in particular the capacity of the state to tame the market.

In modern conditions of globalization, on Fraser's account, the conditioning power of the state framework has gone, and with it the only source of limitation of the powers of the market other than that of people in and of themselves. In

contrast to earlier accounts of the critical potential of the
public sphere, therefore, the efficacy of the transnational
public sphere depends entirely on the actuality and agency
of the 'who' produced by globalization. This 'who' is constituted not by membership or identity but simply by its
inhabiting of the space and time of globalization. It seems
clear, however, that inhabiting the space and time of globalization involves for Fraser a particular kind of lesson learning
from a particular kind of past. It's a past in which the state
did provide, potentially and actually, a mode of limiting the
power of the market that was not in itself hopelessly corrupt
or corrupting. This is a past that is, in practice, shared only
by a minority of all of those currently experiencing the long-
standing effects of economic globalization, and bespeaks a
confidence in a particular account of Western modernity
unlikely to be shared by those who have not been its principal beneficiaries. Fraser's argument relies, in effect, on the
interrelation between transnational powers and transnational publics mirroring the experience internal to a small
number of powerful states over the past two hundred
years. But why would transnational publics trust transnational powers that have predominantly been experienced as
disempowering? And how could transnational publics be
confident that the pattern of relation between legitimacy and
efficacy in these new powers mimicked social-democratic
experiences as opposed to those of authoritarianism or
imperialism?

Conclusion

In bracketing the 'how' and 'translation' questions in her
theory of the changing constitution of 'who' and 'capacity'
conditions within the critical public sphere, Fraser is in
danger of ignoring the extent to which the former are as
embedded in particular theories of the development of the
liberal-capitalist 'metropole' as the latter. She is therefore in
danger of moving too quickly to the conclusion that we
know what the frame is within which dialogue is possible,

essentially the frame of a *present* of globalization that is commonly experienced as novel. This threatens to repeat the mistakes of earlier critical theories of the public sphere which presumed, without acknowledging, the frame of the nation-state. It seems to me that Fraser is right to argue that we need to rethink the frame within which critical public spheres can be theorized, but this rethinking must put modernist theories of history into question, and not presume that there is a smooth transition from Westphalia to post-Westphalia within which all 'dispersed interlocutors' can make sense of their situation and articulate their claims for justice.

References

Fraser, N. (1992) 'Rethinking the Public Sphere: A Contribution to the Critique of Actually Existing Democracy', in C. Calhoun (ed.), *Habermas and the Public Sphere*. Cambridge, MA: MIT Press.

Fraser, N. and N.A. Naples (2004) 'To Interpret the World and to Change It: An Interview with Nancy Fraser', *Signs: Journal of Women, Culture and Society* 29: 1103–24.

Habermas, J. (1989) *The Structural Transformation of the Public Sphere: An Inquiry into a Category of Bourgeois Society*, trans. T. Burger with F. Lawrence. Cambridge: Polity.

Held, D. and A. McGrew (2001) *The Oxford Companion to World Politics*. Oxford: Oxford University Press.

6

Dilemmas of Inclusion
The All-Affected Principle, the All-Subjected Principle, and Transnational Public Spheres

David Owen

The concept of a public sphere as a critical idea refers to a space in which public opinion is mobilized through informal deliberation as a legitimate and effective political force. In the 'classical' theory of the public sphere, 'publicity is supposed to hold officials accountable and to assure that the actions of the state express the will of the citizenry' (Fraser 2007: 7; see also p. 9, this volume). That publicity is primarily understood in terms of this role arguably made a certain degree of sense against a (somewhat idealized) picture of governing constructed in terms of the constitutional-democratic state and the relationship of the state to civil society in which it was assumed that those affected by the domestic laws and polices of the state were the legal members (i.e., nationals) of the state, while the issue of those affected by the foreign policies of the state was typically left unaddressed.[1] Yet, today, as Fraser acutely notes, neither this picture of governing nor its blithe assumptions concerning those affected can be maintained. Consequently, in taking up the question of the place of a critical theory of the public sphere in relation to the increasing transnational contexts of contemporary political life, Nancy Fraser acknowledges the need for a reformulation of the 'classical' view developed by Habermas and his similarly oriented critics (including Fraser herself). Given her characteristic clarity, the features of Fraser's argument immediately relevant to my concerns can be fairly succinctly stated:

1 The critical force of the concept of the public sphere resides in 'the *normative legitimacy* and *political efficiacy* of public opinion', where each of these two basic features is comprised of two elements.

2 Normative legitimacy is predicated on an ideal of *inclusiveness* specified by the principle of all affected interests and an ideal of *equality* specified by the principle of participatory parity.

3 Political efficacy is predicated on the *translation* condition – 'the communicative power generated in civil society must be translated first into binding laws and then into administrative power'– and the *capacity* condition– 'the public power must be able to implement the discursively formed will to which it is responsible' (Fraser 2007: 22; see also p. 31, this volume). In a globalizing world, the implications of these commitments are transformed, not least in terms of who is to be included and how we are to address the fact that we confront important cases of deficits in relation to both democratic legitimacy, most visibly where transnational public powers lack a corresponding public sphere, and political efficacy, most obviously where transnational publics lack a corresponding transnational public power (Fraser 2008: 156).

In this essay, my focus will be on Fraser's struggle with the fundamental difficulty of articulating principles for determining who should be included within transnational publics. I adopt this focus for two reasons. The first is that Fraser has interestingly shifted her position between the initial publication of 'Transnationalizing the Public Sphere' and its reappearance as a chapter in her book *Scales of Justice* in moving her appeal from the all-affected principle to the all-subjected principle – and it is worth clarifying what motivates this shift. The second is that identifying some difficulties that attend Fraser's arguments – whose provisional status she frankly acknowledges – supports the articulation of a more complex normative picture in which I think that her varying intuitions concerning the all-affected and all-subjected principles may be more fully accommodated. In other words, my concern in this essay not so much to criticize Fraser's argument but rather to try to think further through some of the problems that we share.[2] I will conclude by raising some additional questions that arise out of this discussion.

From All-Affected Interests to All-Subjected Persons

In reshaping the issue for normative legitimacy for a critical theory of transnational public spheres, Fraser recognizes that a central problem concerns the issue of who are to be included as fellow members of a public – or, in an alternative formulation which she takes to be identical, as fellow subjects of social justice (2005: 82). Her response to this problem finds a starting-point in the appeal of classical public-sphere theory to the all-affected principle: 'Applying that principle to publicity, it holds that all potentially affected by political decisions should have the chance to participate on terms of parity in the informal processes of opinion formation to which decision-takers should be accountable' (2007: 21; see also p. 29, this volume). Classical public-sphere theory identified those affected by political decisions with the national citizenry of a state, that is, with an approximation of those subject to them. Consequently, as Fraser notes (2007: 20–1; see also p. 28, this volume), it is focused on the issue of parity of participation between national citizens: that is, equal opportunities not only to offer arguments concerning a given political choice but also to shape the agenda and, hence, which issues emerge as topics of political decision-making. In the initial version of her essay, Fraser argued that since 'globalization is driving a widening wedge between affected-ness and political membership', it might make sense that we 'apply the all-affected principle directly to the framing of publicity, without going through the detour of citizenship' (2007: 21; see also p. 30, this volume), where the all-affected principle is specified in terms of the idea that 'what turns a collection of people into fellow members of a public is not shared citizenship, but their co-imbrication in a common set of structures and/or institutions that affect their lives' and arguing, accordingly, that the relevant public for 'any given problem . . . should match the reach of those life-conditioning structures whose effects are at issue' (2007: 22; see also p. 30, this volume). In its later version, Fraser drops this principle in favour of the all-subjected principle, which she glosses in terms of the claim that 'what turns a collection of people into fellow members of a public is not their shared citizenship, or co-imbrication in a causal matrix, but rather their joint subjection to a structure of governance that set[s] the ground rules for their interaction' (2008: 96; see also p. 36, this volume). What motivates this change – and is it justified?

Consider, first, Fraser's ground-breaking article 'Reframing Justice in a Globalizing World' (2005; cf. also 2008: 12–29), in which an appeal to the all-affected principle specified its application in terms of the thought that 'what turns a collection of people into fellow subjects of justice is not geographical proximity, but their co-imbrication in a common structural or institutional framework, which sets the ground rules that govern their social interaction, thereby shaping their respective life possibilities in patterns of advantage and disadvantage' (2005: 82). What is notable about this early formulation is that it seems caught midway between, on the one hand, an appeal to the notion of co-imbrication in a common set of structures and/or institutions as highlighting the salience of subjection to the rules and norms characteristic of these structures and/or institutions (a version of the all-subjected principle) and, on the other, an appeal which highlights the issue of interests which are causally affected by these structures and institutions (a version of the all-affected principle). Fraser's uneasiness concerning the all-affected principle is openly acknowledged in a footnote in which she writes:

> Everything depends on finding a suitable interpretation of the all-affected principle. . . . The problem is that, given the so-called butterfly effect, one can adduce evidence that just about everyone is affected by just about everything. What is needed, therefore, is a way of distinguishing those levels and kinds of effectivity that are sufficient to confer moral standing from those that are not. (2005: 83 fn. 15)

Fraser's initial response to efforts to resolve this problem by theorists such as Carol Gould and David Held is to suggest that there can be a plurality for reasonable interpretations of the principle and, hence, that 'the all-affected principle must be interpreted dialogically, through the give-and-take of argument in democratic deliberation' (2005: 83 fn. 15). However, this response runs straight into the problem of who is to be included in this process of democratic deliberation that will decide on a politically legitimate interpretation of the all-affected principle. Although Fraser does not consider the issue further, one might be tempted here by the thought of a two-level model in which everyone should be included in deliberating over which interpretation of the all-affected principle will be applied in framing the conditions of inclusiveness of publics within this global frame, where the justification for such global inclusion would be grounded on the normative fact that all are affected by a decision concerning how the conditions of inclusion for publics are to be demarcated. The difficulty with such a proposal is that it would tendentiously pre-empt the issue, if there are a plurality of reasonable interpretations of the all-affected principle, of which interpretation is most appropriate for a given case.

By the time that she writes 'Abnormal Justice', Fraser has come to see several problems with the all-affected principle:

Aiming to conceptualize *transnational* justice, proponents of the *all-affected principle* propose to resolves debates about the 'who' by appealing to social relations of interdependence. For them, accordingly, what makes a group of people fellow subjects of justice is their objective co-imbrication in a web of causal relationships. . . . This approach has the merit of providing a critical check on self-serving notions of membership, while also taking cognizance of social relations. Yet, by conceiving relations objectivistically, in terms of causality, it effectively relegates the choice of the 'who' to mainstream social science. In addition, the all-affected principle falls prey to the *reduction ad absurdum* of the butterfly effect, which holds that everyone is affected by everything. Unable to identify *morally relevant* social relations, it has trouble resisting the one-size-fits-all globalism it sought to avoid. (2008: 64, original emphasis)

With refreshing candour, Fraser acknowledges that she had seen the all-affected principle as the most promising candidate for answering the question 'who counts?', but has come to 'believe that these difficulties are so serious that the better course of wisdom is to abandon the all-affected principle' (2008: 179 fn. 29) in favour of *the all-subjected principle*, which, as we have noted, she glosses as the claim that what makes people into fellow subjects of justice is 'their joint subjection to a structure of governance that sets the ground rules that govern their interaction' (2008: 65; note the uptake of her earlier – 2005: 82 – ambiguous formulation of the all-affected principle). But how compelling are these criticisms of the all-affected principle?

The Critique of the All-Affected Interests Principle

Consider, first, the issue of the 'butterfly effect'. As I understand this notion, it refers to the high sensitivity of complex dynamic systems to variations in initial conditions such that small variations in initial conditions can produce large-scale variations in the overall behaviour of the system – and, hence, in complex systems, since one can never fully accurately describe the initial conditions, one cannot offer predictions of overall system behaviour beyond the short term (as the history of weather forecasting amply demonstrates). So the thought for our concerns would be that a single action – say, my failing to vote in a local election – in the complex system of global human interaction could be an essential part of the initial conditions that eventually generate a major event within the system – say, global revolution. Suppose that this is true in respect of global human interaction, why does this matter? The truth, if it is one, that any action, however trivial, may (or even will) affect the interests of all in the long term has no necessary relationship to the claim that all should be included in all decisions about everything, and this is precisely because the causal relationship is epistemically untrackable. The all-affected principle is a moral, not a metaphysical, principle. The butterfly effect may mark a significant epistemic limitation on the spatial or temporal range of our capacity to track which interests are affected by what, but it seems to me that this is neither a normative objection to the principle nor sufficient grounds to conclude that it issues in a 'one-size-fits-all' globalism. What the butterfly effect does raise as a critical topic is the question of how we respond to this limitation, where this is not simply a question of what social-scientific tools we have available for constructing plausible accounts of, or counterfactuals concerning, who is potentially affected by particular actions or decisions.

This point brings us to Fraser's second criticism, namely, that 'by conceiving relations objectivistically, in terms of causality, it [the all-affected principle] effectively relegates the choice of the "who" to mainstream social science' (2008: 65). It may be useful here to consider an analogy with issues of outcome responsibility, which, since it also involves reference to a causal chain, confronts the issue of our epistemic limitations in the same way. Thus, as David Miller notes, in distinguishing causal and outcome responsibility:

> Causal responsibility is being invoked when we ask the question 'why did O occur?' We want to know which among the

many conditions that had to be fulfilled in order for O to occur to single out as the cause of O. As Hart and Honoré among others have pointed out, there is no single correct answer to this question. . . . In the case of outcome responsibility, our interest is different. We want to know whether a particular agent can be credited or debited with a particular outcome – a gain or loss, either to the agent herself or to other parties. . . . Because the underlying notion is of an outcome being credited or debited to the agent, the nature of the causal chain matters for such attributions of responsibility. *As the chain becomes longer and more tortuous, responsibility dissipates.* (2007: 86–8, my italics)

It is for this reason that we typically take ourselves to be justified only in holding agents responsible for the consequences of their actions that are reasonably foreseeable. However, and this is the critical point, we may justifiably vary the relevant standards of responsibility in terms of, for example, the degree of voluntariness of the action and the degree of foreseeability of consequences in relation to the moral significance of the interests affected – and, as such, judgements concerning attributions of outcome responsibility cannot be relegated to mainstream social science. I suggest that a similar point holds in relation to the all-affected principle in that we may justifiably limit those included to those where we can reasonably assign significant probability values to their salient interests being affected, yet we may also reasonably vary the criteria of inclusiveness in terms of varying the probability values that we adopt in relation to the degree of moral significance of the interests affected. On such a view, application of the all-affected principle cannot be relegated to mainstream social science any more than can attributions of outcome responsibility.

Fraser's third criticism recalls the well-known point that, as a formal principle, the all-affected principle is indiscriminate in terms of its consideration of morally significant, insignificant, and abhorrent interests. This is not really an objection to the principle, however; rather it is a reminder that we need some independently justifiable standards to demarcate the interests that should count as morally (or politically) significant in particular contexts. This might seem to raise a specific problem for the type of critical theory advanced by Fraser (and, for that matter, Rainer Forst), since this type of theory holds that standards of justice cannot be specified independently of a political dialogue between the affected parties – a conceptual claim that appears to threaten the prospect of a vicious circle. However, since even the most dialogical account specifies certain basic moral requirements as founding conditions of reasonable dialogue, the problem of circularity can be addressed by using these basic moral norms to specify a range of fundamental interests that count in determining an initial public, while allowing for dialogical development and, hence, expansive transformations of those included in the public as the further (reflexively revisable) standards of justice and/or political legitimacy emerge. Indeed, Fraser's adopts just such a thought in her appeals to the notion of 'good-enough deliberation' (2008: 45).

Fraser's final objection to the all-affected principle is that it slips into 'one-size-fits-all globalism'. Although I have resisted the butterfly effect argument to this conclusion, the same outcome can be reached by another route. The difficulty for the all-affected principle is that who is potentially affected depends on what we may call *the decision-space* of the polity. In its narrowest construal, the decision-space is constituted by the options on the table at a given time between which the decision-takers are to choose. Hence, in a decision context in which there are three mutually exclusive options, A, B, and C, those potentially affected would include all whose interests would be affected by the choice of A or B or C rather than either of the alternatives. However, since Fraser's condition of participatory parity requires that those included must be able to deliberate not merely over choices but also over the agendas within which choices are framed, a consistent application of the all-affected principle would require construing the decision-space of a polity in terms of all the possible options that could be chosen under any possible agenda – a position for which Goodin (2007) has recently argued and which, as he notes, entails that those whose interests are potentially affected include pretty much everyone. If this argument is right, then it seems that Fraser's worry that appeal to the all-affected principle slides straight into a 'one-size-fits-all globalism' is justified.[3] This is a worry for Fraser from the standpoint of a *critical theory* of the public sphere since the all-affected principle is consequently radically unmoored from any sociological grounding in actual transnational social and political relations in their diverse contemporary forms. Instead of a critical theory, on this view, the all-affected principle leaves us simply with an abstract moralized standpoint.

Insofar as the all-affected principle leads to these conclusions, Fraser's commitment to a critical theory of the public sphere appears sufficient to motivate and justify her turn to the all-subjected principle. However, her presentation of this principle is not without difficulties of its own – and I will turn now to address this topic by taking up two issues for her argument.

The All-Subjected Persons Principle

The first issue concerns the conditions of being subject to a structure of governance. Fraser wisely adopts an ecumenical view of governance that encompasses states and non-state actors that generate 'enforceable rules that structure important swaths of social interaction' (2008: 65); however, I think that what is left out of Fraser's account is the importance of an acknowledgement of different types of subjection to structures of governance that may come into play depending on the character of the structure of governance in question. Thus, for example, even in the very simple case of a purely territorial bounded polity in which membership is specified by habitual residence, there will be two distinct types of subjection and sets of coercive norms in play. First, there will be the subjection of those who are habitually resident on the territory of the polity and, hence, subject to its rule in respect of the norms through which it regulates their relations to one another. Second, there will be the subjection of those who are involuntarily excluded from habitual residence on the territory of the polity and, hence, subject to its rule in respect of the enforceable norms through which it demarcates members and non-members (Abizadeh, 2008). (The types of subjection are further differentiated in relation to complex structures of governance such as states which combine territorial and national elements.) The crucial point here is that for any non-global structure of governance, there will always be at least two distinct publics constituted – the public comprised of members and the public comprised of members and those involuntarily excluded from membership – which take as their respective foci coercive norms governing the relations of members and coercive norms governing access to membership.

It might be objected that Fraser is addressing inclusion in a public rather than issues of formal membership of a polity or structure of governance. There are two responses to such an objection. The first is that it is irrelevant since one can rephrase the relevant distinction as one between those subject to the norms governing *who is governed* by a structure of governance and those subject to norms governing *how 'those who are governed' are governed* by a structure of governance. The second response is to note that it is, I think, implicit within Fraser's argument that part of the answer to the question of *how* to address the problems of a transnational public sphere is the generation of new modes and rules of political membership.[4]

This first critical point poses no significant problems for Fraser's argument; it simply elaborates or supplements it. The second problem, although not specific to Fraser's reflections on the all-subjected principle, does pose a significant problem for this principle. The problem at stake relates to the normative significance of the fact that decisions taken through a structure of governance may have significant causal effects on the basic interests of people who do not fall (formally or informally) within the scope of the coercive power of the structure of governance – and, for all the problems of the all-affected principle, it is unclear such individuals (or social groups) should be denied a political voice in relation to those decisions. (It is, in other words, unclear why they could not reasonably respond to offers couched in the other standard way of dealing with negative externalities, i.e., compensation to those affected, that such an offer is an insult to their standing as moral and political agents.) Although this problem is not specific to Fraser's version of the all-subjected principle, one might reasonably think that the issue is a particularly sensitive one for her precisely because she is so acutely alert to problems of 'misframing' in relation to issues of transnational justice – and, indeed, has done much of the fundamental conceptual work needed to make these issues visible in a theoretically perspicuous way. Given this, let me offer two theoretically distinct routes by which the problem may be overcome.

The first route involves reintroducing the all-affected principle as playing a role which is distinct from that of the all-subjected principle. To sketch this route, we may begin with a context in which the all-subjected principle does not seem well placed to provide us with guidance, namely, a context characterized by the absence of institutions of governance regarding some set or complex of social relations. In such a context, two questions may arise. First, should the social relations concerned be governed? And, second, who should answer the first question? These questions are related by the all-affected principle. The answer to the first depends on identifying whether the social relations at issue are such that they give rise to, or are reproduced through, actions by some individuals (or groups) which affect the morally significant interests of other individuals (or groups) – as may be the case, for example, if they live in territorial proximity or share membership of a national community – and, hence, give rise to a common interest in the question of the governance of such social relations. The answer to the second question is 'all those whose morally significant interests are interlinked through these social relations'. Thus, the role of the all-affected principle is to specify who should be involved in publics concerned with *constructing* structures of governance, whereas the all-subjected principle identifies who should be included in the publics which hold accountable *constructed* structures of governance. Consequently, those whose morally significant interests are affected by certain types of decisions by states, for example, are entitled to inclusion within a public that considers whether or not such decisions on the part of these actors should be subject to governance.

The second route does not involve recourse to the all-affected principle but, rather, operating solely with the all-subjected principle, advances the claim that the polities of, structures of governance of, and relations between these governmental entities that compose the contemporary global political order can themselves be seen as comprising a regime of global governance. Consequently, those whose interests are affected in morally significant ways by the decisions of any given structure of governance but who are not themselves part of this particular structure of governance have, on the basis of their subjection to the regime of global governance, an entitlement to inclusion within a global public in which the moral costs and political legitimacy of this current global ordering of governance can be addressed.

Each of these options has advantages and disadvantages. The second is more theoretically simple in form and allows Fraser to maintain the all-subjected principle as simultaneously grounding membership of a public and being a subject of justice; its more controversial move comes in the claim that the ordering of global politics can itself be addressed as a 'centre-less' structure of governance. The first option is theoretically messier, although it has the advantage of accommodating the intuition that being affected in morally significant ways by the actions or decisions of others matters independently of whether we are co-subjects of a structure of governance. The theoretical difficulty raised by the incorporation of both principles into a more complex picture is this: Which principle grounds our standing as subjects of justice? My own provisional view, although I don't have the space to elaborate or defend it here, is that what grounds being a subject of justice is being subject to power (where both having one's interest affected as a causal result of another's decisions and being subject to a structure of governance are varieties of being subject to power). On this view, as Forst (2012) argues, the fundamental form of being a subject of justice is an entitlement to a basic right to justification in respect of the relations and effects of power to which one is subject, yet where the different ways in which one is subject to power generate different responses to questions concerning the scope and focus of the right to justification. Thus, in respect of those subject to a structure of governance, the scope and focus of the right to justification are given by the question of how to govern the relations of those subject to governance (e.g., issues of social justice); whereas in relation to those whose interests are affected, the scope and focus of the right to justification are given by the question of whether to subject to governance the social relations that causally generate the effects in question. (This is likely to be, in part, a debate about whether the effects are best construed as misfortune or injustice, and where that line is drawn, as Judith Shklar acutely observed, a political choice [1990: 5].) It will be clear from these remarks that my own preference is for the theoretically messier option that gives the all-affected and all-subjected principles distinct roles to play in a critical theory of the public sphere and, more generally, in a critical theory of transnational justice – and this is, not least, because I share much of what I take to be Fraser's intuitive sense of the salience of both of these principles.

Conclusion

The very limited goal of this essay has been to try to elaborate some of the difficulties that attend working out principles of inclusion for a critical theory of the transnational public sphere – and to offer some provisional suggestions for resolving these difficulties. In this respect, I have not addressed the larger questions concerning whether, for example, in the context of networks of governance that link agencies, be they public, private, or quasi-public, the model provided by the classical theory of the public sphere is too governmental to be appropriate to issues of transnational governance – this is a serious issue which requires considerably more attention, but, whatever the answer to such questions, the question of who comprises the public will remain a fundamental normative issue.

Notes

1 In this respect, the classical theory seems closer to the all-subjected principle than to the all-affected principle, despite its official commitment to the latter.

2 My own trajectory is slightly different to that of Fraser since I started with a commitment to the all-subjected principle on the basis that it addresses the fundamental political relation of being governed – a view that I offered in 'Resistance in Movement: Migration, Legitimacy and Global Governance', which was given as a plenary lecture to the Philosophy and Social Sciences Conference, Czech Institute for Philosophy/Academy of Sciences, May 2005, which, by remarkable synchronicity, was the day after Nancy Fraser gave the paper 'Abnormal Justice' as a plenary lecture. However, I have come to think that the all-affected principle may have a role to play as well – as I will clarify in the final section of this essay.

3 I think it may be possible to block Goodin's move to 'one-size-fits-all globalism' if we distinguish between having an interest in membership of a polity or structure of governance and having an interest in a decision taken by that polity. Considered as a criterion for specifying a unit for collective decision-making, the all-affected principle points to the importance of the intermeshed interests of persons, arguing that 'common reciprocal interests in one another's action and choices are what makes these groups [e.g., territorial, historical, national] appropriate units for collective decision-making' (Goodin, 2007: 48). In other words, having an interest in membership of the public of a polity or structure of governance is predicated not on one's interests being affected by some (possible or actual) decision of *that* polity but, rather, on one's interests being intermeshed with

the interests of others and, hence, the fact that one has an interest in common with these others of being a member of the political community that regulates the relations between the members of this community. Notice, though, that this is a *recursive* principle in the sense that while persons whose interests are affected by a decision made by a given polity do not thereby have an interest in membership of the public of that first-order polity, in virtue of having an interest affected by a decision of that polity they do have a common interest with all other persons affected by that decision (including those who are members of the first-order polity) in membership of the public of a second-order polity or structure of governance that has powers to regulate the decision made by the first-order polity. Once we have seen this, the move to one-size-fits-all globalism is blocked.

4 I have elsewhere addressed some of the issues of contemporary political membership (Owen 2010). Important work on this topic can be found in, for example, Baubock 1994, 2003, 2005, 2007; Lopez-Guerra 2005; Rubio-Marin 2000, 2006.

References

Abizadeh, A. (2008) 'Democratic Theory and Border Coercion', *Political Theory* 36(1): 37–65.

Baubock, R. (1994) *Transnational Citizenship*. London: Edward Elgar.

Baubock, R. (2003) 'Towards a Political Theory of Migrant Transnationalism', *International Migration Review* 37: 700–23.

Baubock, R. (2005) 'Expansive Citizenship – Voting beyond Territory and Membership', *Political Science and Policy* 38: 683–7.

Baubock, R. (2007) 'Stakeholder Citizenship and Transnational Political Participation: A Normative Evaluation of External Voting', *Fordham Law Review* 75: 2393–447.

Fraser, N. (2005) 'Reframing Justice in a Globalizing World', *New Left Review* 36(Nov.–Dec.): 69–88.

Fraser, N. (2007) 'Transnationalizing the Public Sphere: On the Legitimacy and Efficacy of Public Opinion in a Post-Westphalian World',*Theory, Culture & Society* 24(4): 7–30.

Fraser, N. (2008) *Scales of Justice: Reimaging Political Space in a Globalizing World*. Cambridge: Polity.

Forst, R. (2012) *The Right to Justification*, trans. J. Flynn, New York: Columbia University Press.

Goodin, R.E. (2007) 'Enfranchising All Affected Interests, and Its Alternatives', *Philosophy and Public Affairs* 35: 40–68.

Lopez-Guerra, C. (2005) 'Should Expatriates Vote?', *Journal of Political Philosophy* 13: 216–34.

Miller, D. (2007) *National Responsibility and Global Justice*. Oxford: Oxford University Press.

Owen, D. (2010) 'Resident Aliens, Non-Resident Citizens and Voting Rights: Towards a Pluralist Theory of Transnational Political Equality and Modes of Political Belonging', in G. Calder, P. Cole, and J. Seglow (eds), *Citizenship Acquisition and National Belonging: Migration, Membership and the Liberal Democratic State*. Basingstoke: Palgrave.

Rubio-Marin, R. (2000) *Immigration as a Democratic Challenge*. Cambridge: Cambridge University Press.

Rubio-Marin, R. (2006) 'Transnational Politics and the Democratic Nation-State: Normative Challenges of Expatriate Voting Rights and Nationality Retention of Emigrants', *New York University Law Review* 11: 117–47.

Shklar, J. (1990) *The Faces of Injustice*. New Haven: Yale University Press.

7

Publicity, Subjection, Critique
A Reply to My Critics

Nancy Fraser

for Edward J. Snowden and Private Manning,
heroes of transnational publicity,
in gratitude and with admiration

A lot has happened since I wrote 'Transnationalizing the Public Sphere' in 2007. The crisis of 2008 threw into bold relief the global supremacy of finance capital, its power to wreck economies, dislocate societies, dictate policy, and bring elected governments to their knees – all without even a nod to public opinion, which it cavalierly brushed aside with a flick of the wrist. Regional bodies, such as the European Union, once touted as avatars of transnational democracy, dismally failed to bring private power to public heel; capitulating cravenly to investors and shifting the costs onto working people, they ordered draconian cuts in public spending, ignored massive protests, and forfeited democratic legitimacy. Across the Atlantic, meanwhile, the first black president of the United States, elected on a wave of anti-Bush revulsion, continued 'the war on terror'; vastly expanding the security state and fiercely resisting public oversight of executive power, he mercilessly hounded whistleblowers who exposed its secret surveillance for all to see. At the same time, as if on a parallel track, subaltern counterpublics flexed their muscle across the globe; utilizing new media, they helped unleash a major transnational cascade of activist protest, which occupied public squares and toppled authoritarian regimes, but failed to transform 'deep states' or structures of governance, which have remained overwhelmingly captive to the powers-that-be.[1]

Taken together, these developments vindicate my diagnosis in 'Transnationalizing the Public Sphere'. Today, even more clearly than in 2007, the basic preconditions of democratic publicity are unfulfilled. The governments of territorially bounded states, however democratic, are severely overmatched by transnational private powers, like finance capital, and by a declining global hegemon, the United States, which dictate the basic terms under which we live. Nor can those forces of domination be brought to account by even the most vigilant national publics, which lack the necessary reach and heft. Transnational public spheres could fare better in this regard, but only if two conditions were met: first, they would need to be sufficiently inclusive and solidaristic to ensure parity of participation among far-flung interlocutors who are disparately situated, ideologically diverse, and unequally empowered; and, second, they would need appropriate addressees – robust, accountable transnational public institutions, able to transmute public opinion into enforceable political will. Today, however, as in 2007, neither condition holds. Actually existing transnational publics do not meet standards of normative legitimacy; and absent the requisite addressees, the opinion they generate lacks practical efficacy. In short, the stars of public-sphere theory do not align. Mismatches of scale among public spheres, political institutions, and private powers derail its fundamental premise: that communicative power, generated through unrestricted, inclusive discussion in civil society, could tame administrative power and, through it, overcome domination, subjecting the forces that govern our lives to democratic control.

If recent developments vindicate this diagnosis, they also suggest a deepening crisis of public-sphere theory. At first sight, this crisis appears as a widening chasm between the theory's ideals and social reality. But that formulation understates the difficulty. Not resolvable simply by 'narrowing the gap', the trouble goes to the very heart of public-sphere theory – and of the 'Westphalian' paradigm of democratic theory to which it belongs. We are no longer faced today, as Jürgen Habermas once thought we were, with the manipulation of public opinion in political communities whose boundaries can be taken as given. Rather, we confront such problems now, at a moment of structural crisis, when domination is exercised openly at multiple scales, when political membership and public standing are hotly contested, and when the contours of democratic politics are no longer clear. Today, in other words, we can no longer easily envision, as Habermas once thought he could, a set of arrangements in which public opinion could be normatively legitimate and practically efficacious at the same time. Worse still, we lack a clear sense of what legitimacy and efficacy could possibly mean in the emphatically *post*-Westphalian conjuncture we now inhabit.

How should theorists of publicity respond to this situation? Should we accept that present mismatches among publics, institutions, and powers are inevitable? That public opinion in a globalizing world simply cannot be normatively legitimate and practically efficacious? Effectively bowing to present-day social reality, should we abandon the project of a *critical theory* of democratic publicity, which grounds its norms immanently, in the history of the present, identifying emancipatory potentials and clarifying prospects for overcoming domination? Should we retreat instead to ideal theorizing, which marks the tragic unbridgeable gulf between 'is' and 'ought'? Or should we lower our sights, forswearing overly stringent principles of legitimacy and efficacy in favour of feasible, realistic alternatives? Or, finally, should we follow the more arduous path I outlined in 2007 and try to reconstruct the critical theory of the public sphere in a form adequate to the post-Westphalian contours of the twenty-first century?

Variants of each of these strategies can be found in the responses to my essay collected here. To be sure, none of the contributors openly advocates abandoning critical theory; all of them endorse its signature project of locating the tension 'between fact and norm' historically, grasping both horns of the dilemma, and working it through. Yet some of the critics end up surrendering that aspiration; whether by prioritizing feasibility or by privileging utopian ideals, they fail to keep hold simultaneously of legitimacy and efficacy. Effectively, these responses illustrate a potentially devastating claim made by some contributors: even as I diagnosed the mismatches of scale that bedevil public-sphere theory, my essay radically underestimated the difficulties involved in reconstructing it.

Taken together, therefore, the responses collected here pose a major challenge to my position: Is it really possible to envision a critical theory of democratic publicity for the twenty-first century? I aim in what follows to respond to this challenge as best I can – by systematically working through the arguments of each contributor.

Transnationalizing the Westphalian Frame?

One approach to salvaging public-sphere theory prioritizes the context in which it originally developed and historically flourished: namely, the modern territorial state. This approach has the weight of history and commonsense on its side. After all, if public opinion has ever served anywhere as a genuine democratizing force, it has surely been within the bounded political communities of the modern Westphalian state system. Only within those contexts has anything approaching unrestricted, inclusive discussion in civil society managed to generate a body of opinion that could plausibly claim to be 'public' in the sense of expressing the general interest. Only on the national scale, moreover, has such opinion ever remotely succeeded in bending institutionalized power to popular will. Only when framed in national terms, finally, as an expression of shared citizenship, has the ideal of democratic publicity ever acquired any real social traction, informing the hopes and expectations of real social subjects. What could be more sensible, then, than to tackle the crisis of public-sphere theory by reasserting the primacy of the national frame?

Nick Couldry pursues an approach of this sort. Aiming to adapt the venerable national framing of publicity to the new post-Westphalian condition, he centres his intervention on a contrast between two scenarios. One scenario, attributed to me, features a *transnational* public sphere, wholly new, constructed from scratch, and delinked from national publics. The other, embraced by him, figures a *transnationalized* public sphere, created by stretching existing national publics to incorporate migrant perspectives and extra-domestic concerns. For Couldry, the second scenario is preferable on two counts. Conceptually, the approach attributed to me implausibly envisions 'the' transnational public sphere as 'one single, continuous space or entity' located beyond and disconnected from national publics, while his 'transnationalized' alternative aptly assumes a network of multiple publics, interlinked and inhabiting different scales (p. 48). Practically, moreover, the first (transnation*al*) scenario is so removed from people's existing habits and identifications as to be politically unfeasible and is likely to divert us 'from the points within *existing* national and local public spheres where pressures of transnationalization need to and can, more plausibly, be addressed' (p. 44, original emphasis). The better course, according to Couldry, is to start from where and who we already are (national citizens of territorial states who get our news mainly from the national media and address our claims chiefly to the national state) and proceed to work outwards from there. The goal should be, not a transnational, but a *transnationalized* public sphere.

Let us pass quickly over some unfortunate interpretive missteps: that I never advocated the building *de novo* of a single, unitary transnational public sphere, disconnected from other communicative spaces; that I am, on the contrary, among the originators of the idea of multiple publics linked up in a communicative network spanning different scales; that in calling my essay 'Transnationalizing the Public Sphere', my primary objective was to reconstruct public-sphere theory, not to re-engineer social reality; that my stance there was not prescriptive but critical-theoretical, aimed less at sketching an ideal state of affairs than at probing contemporary tensions between fact and norm.

Let us focus instead on the underlying orientation of Couldry's argument, which prioritizes feasibility. Writing as a media sociologist, he seeks in part to correct the empirical record, insisting (quite plausibly) that public communication today remains largely a national affair. But Couldry is also bent on making a strategic point: given the robustness of the national frame, it is folly to invest one's energies anywhere else. Realism demands that we set aside at least for now the unpleasant fact that national debate in wealthy countries cannot give adequate voice to the global poor, those distant subject populations whose life prospects mightily depend on decisions taken outside their borders, in the capitalist core. For those populations to agitate now, in transnational publics, against the offshore agents of their dispossession, is to pursue a will-o'-the-wisp. Nor should we dwell too much on the inconvenient fact that, even in the states of the core, national policy is strictly constrained by transnational powers, which neither national publics nor national states can hope to control. To try to confront those powers now, by mobilizing communicative counterpower at a comparable scale, is to tilt at windmills. It is better, in sum, because 'easier', to tweak existing national public spheres.

Four points strike me as crucial in evaluating this argument. First, Couldry assumes that his domestic-centred strategy affords a possible, if lengthy, path to the long-term goal we presumably share of a world in which public opinion can be democratically legitimate and practically efficacious in shaping transnational processes in the interests of all. But this assumption is doubtful, given the historically sedimented interest of wealthy countries in defending privileges they enjoy off the backs of the global poor. If the assumption fails, moreover, and this is my second point, then Couldry's approach would amount in the end to abandoning critical theory. Treating existing empirical conditions as inevitable givens, he would be counselling us to lower our sights – to accept the dominance of the national frame, to forswear as utopian direct transnational mobilization against transnational domination, and to focus our energies instead on attainable goals. The effect of such a 'realistic' posture would be to eliminate, rather than work through, the tension between fact and norm. However, and this is my third point, this sort of realism positivistically misconstrues the 'facts' by abstracting them from 'possibilities' – and from the broader historical processes within which their meaning unfolds. A critical approach would start from the contradictory character of our times: from the equally evident 'facts' that transnational public spheres already exist, alongside their more entrenched national counterparts: that they already communicate with the latter to some extent; that some of them are currently serving as platforms for mounting critiques, however outgunned, of neoliberal finance, corporate capital, and US hegemony; that some of them already offer a measure of voice, however subordinate, to segments of the global poor. If we combine these 'facts' with those introduced by Couldry, then we come to my fourth and last point: there is no compelling reason to choose between his preferred scenario and the one he attributes to me. Nothing precludes our working simultaneously to transnationalize existing national public spheres, to develop (or even create) transnational publics, and to forge linkages among them. On the contrary, it is only through this sort of both/and strategy that we can have any hope of enhancing both the legitimacy and the efficacy of public opinion in a globalizing world.

Democratization by Network Power?

A second approach to the crisis of public-sphere theory prioritizes the transnational frame. Uncowed by republican pieties, this approach prides itself on clear-eyed recognition of the real face of power in the present constellation: a network of global governance institutions, comprising not only the usual suspects (the World Bank, the International Monetary Fund, the Bank of International Settlements, the International Atomic Energy Agency, NATO, and various agencies of the United Nations), but also others, more obscure, yet highly consequential. Like states, these institutions make coercively enforceable rules that govern broad swathes of social interaction among many people. Unlike states, however, they are neither authorized by nor accountable to those subject to their decisions. Elite-dominated, neo-imperial, beholden to capital and to geopolitical might, they possess a *modus operandi* that is expressly designed to evade the force of public opinion and to bypass political control by any *demos*. This real world of technocratic, neoliberal global governance is fundamentally out of sync with a public-sphere theory scaled to the Westphalian state. Only a scaled-up framework, committed to theorizing the conditions for mobilizing publicity transnationally, can fulfil the mandate of critical theory under current conditions.

Kate Nash aims to develop such a framework. Unlike Couldry, she proposes to focus on communications communities that overrun the borders of Westphalian states. For her, the privileged objects of consideration are 'transnational advocacy networks' (TANs) clustered around global governance institutions, whose operations they subject to scrutiny and seek to influence. It is here, she contends, in the world of international nongovernmental organization policy expertise, that a functional equivalent of democratic publicity can be discerned. Like public spheres, TANs serve to bring decision-makers to account; pressing for policies responsive to the needs of the global poor, they effectively help to democratize global governance. Like Couldry's, however, this approach requires recalibrating the normative bar. As Nash is careful to note, TANs themselves are undemocratic, non-representative, and non-inclusive; they purport to speak for, but do not speak with, the global poor. If the opinion they generate cannot as a result claim normative legitimacy, it nevertheless embodies another virtue, so far overlooked in public-sphere theory. TANs manifest the quality of 'usefulness': enhancing the responsiveness of global governance, while bettering the lives of the global poor, these undemocratic networks serve as agents of democratization. If that sounds paradoxical, one should consider this: rethinking publicity through the prism of TANs is a way of grounding public-sphere theory's norms immanently, in a diagnosis of current conditions. Not content simply to apply inherited Westphalian norms to present-day post-Westphalian facts, Nash effectively reverses the direction of analysis. By interrogating a new form of discursive practice, she derives a new norm of democratic publicity.

Nash's argument has the merit of directly confronting the transnational face of power in the present era. But her effort to scale up public-sphere theory is fraught with difficulties. For starters, the proposal to treat TANs as functional equivalents of public spheres is counterintuitive. After all, as Nash concedes, these arenas are elite professional networks often dependent on corporate funding and dominated by voices from the Global North. Thus, their deliberations are far from public in the sense of being in principle open to all – far less so, if truth be told, than the mainstream Westphalian arenas championed by Couldry. Nor is it clear that TANs are efficacious in constraining institutionalized power. Certainly, they have not succeeded to date in altering global policy to the benefit of the global poor – and for reasons that are not accidental. Absent links to external mass mobilization, any radical proposals their members advance are sure to be quickly dismissed. Whatever sway they manage to assert is more a matter of insider influence than communicative power. Under these conditions, even the best-intentioned experts are liable to become ensnared by the power structure. TANs are far less likely to transform transnational governance than to be co-opted by it.

It is no doubt this double deficit (of normative legitimacy and practical efficacy) that prompts Nash to revisit the norms of publicity. Contending that Habermasian principles are too stringent for current conditions, she proposes to introduce the new norm of 'usefulness' into public-sphere theory. This notion, as I understand it, is meant to capture the paradoxical idea that a non-democratic communicative process can have democratizing effects. The thought, I suppose, is that, by working to improve anti-poverty policies, TAN members may help to establish the material conditions through which the global poor could someday exercise political voice on their own behalf. But is this really plausible? One worry is that the purported usefulness of TANs depends on their being efficacious, a supposition I have just suggested is open to doubt. Another is that treating people as policy objects is by no means the surest route to empowering them as political subjects. On the contrary, modern history is replete with top-down redistributive projects – liberal, communist, nationalist, populist – which failed to enhance democratic participation in the slightest degree.

On this last point, it is instructive to contrast TANs to the feminist counterpublics I discussed in my 1990 essay, 'Rethinking the Public Sphere' (reprinted as Fraser 1992). Although Nash invokes these subaltern communicative spaces as prior exemplars of usefulness, comparable to TANs, I find the divergences more significant than the similarities. Unlike TANs, second-wave feminist counterpublics comprised the agitational wing of a radical mass social movement – emancipatory, anti-systemic, and committed to structural change. Dedicated at once to external propaganda and to internal consciousness-raising, these were discourse arenas in which members of a subordinated gender learned to speak for themselves and to talk back to power. Unlike TANs, they can plausibly be considered democratizing, but not because they were useful in Nash's sense. Rather, their democratizing force lay, first, in their capacity to mitigate, if not overcome, women's marginalization (and in some cases exclusion) from public debate; and, second, in their ability to lift some major restrictions on what could count as a public issue, redrawing the boundaries between public and private and shattering taboos that had served to enforce male

domination. Thus, feminist subaltern counterpublics func-
tioned to enhance the democratic legitimacy of public opinion
by *enlarging the public*, admitting new voices and new topics
of discussion.

I draw three conclusions from these reflections. First, usefulness is not a useful idea for public-sphere theory. Far from
representing a new principle of democratic publicity, its
content is parasitic on the theory's familiar norms of legitimacy and efficacy. Second, and more disturbing, the idea
serves chiefly in Nash's text as an alibi for the shortcomings
of TANs, a way of prettifying discursive arenas that fail to
meet those classical norms. But if that is right – and this is
my third conclusion, then Nash ends up in a position close
to Couldry's. Lowering the bar, she, too, prioritizes feasibility, even as she, too, proposes a scenario that fails to embody
it. The result flies in the face of her best intentions: despite
her efforts to theorize immanently, from within the belly of
the global beast, Nash eliminates the tension between fact
and norm. She, too, abandons the project of a *critical theory*
of the public sphere.

From *Demos* to Multitude?

What other strategies remain for reimagining public-sphere
theory in the current conjuncture? A third approach follows
Nash in prioritizing the transnational frame, while jettison-
ing her technocratic elitism. Distrustful of global governance
institutions, and of the expert communities entangled with
them, this approach looks to anti-systemic movements as
agents of transformation. Valorizing the independent mili-
tancy of Occupy, WikiLeaks, and the World Social Forum,
it affirms efforts to build counterhegemonic centres of
opinion and will formation, far removed from circuits of
institutionalized power. Aiming to evade the hierarchical
logic of administrative rule, it seeks to reconstruct public-
sphere theory in a way that gives pride of place to autonomous direct action by subaltern counterpublics and 'strong'
(decision-making) publics in civil society. Where else, after

all, are we likely to find democratizing forces that can advance the theory's ideals under current conditions?

Fuyuki Kurasawa pursues an approach of this type. Naming his framework 'anarchist cosmopolitanism', he rejects schemes that would democratize global governance by transferring the powers of rogue institutions to transnational parliaments, accountable to transnational publics and electorates, charged with reining in private power and with regulating common affairs on a global scale. For Kurasawa, that strategy cannot empower autonomous public opinion. On the contrary, it is in the nature of formal institutions, whether national, transnational, or global, to functionalize input from civil society, incorporating the latter into the autopoietic processes by which they maintain and expand their own power. Only a project of 'engaged withdrawal' from the institutions of global governance can evade the logic of co-optation. Only the 'concretization of counterpublicity' in self-organized collectives and self-managed councils can dispel heteronomy, restoring capacities for self-determination, alienated to external governing powers, to their rightful subjects. To realize the ideals of public-sphere theory requires, in sum, that we abandon the political project associated with it. Instead of mobilizing public opinion to influence public authorities, we should circumvent the latter altogether, averting co-optation through stealth and cultivating autonomous action to transform social arrangements from the bottom up.

Kurasawa's approach sounds breathtakingly radical. Raising questions that transcend the current conjuncture, even as they surface acutely within it, he proposes to alter the deep grammar of public-sphere theory. The latter has always assumed a two-track model of politics: on a first, informal track, autonomous publics in civil society generate public opinion, while on a second, formal track, political institutions make authorized binding decisions and carry them out. The theory's chief claim, of course, concerns the relation between the two tracks: conditional on free communication between them, democracy requires that the second track channel the first, empowering public opinion by translating the discursively generated sense of the general interest into binding decisions and authorized action. Kurasawa rejects such arrangements. Given a foothold, he claims, the administrative logics of the political system are bound to colonize the independent energies of civil society. To emancipate the latter, one must eliminate formal institutions. But that implies an entirely different model, premised on a *single-track* understanding of democratic politics.

To assess Kurasawa's argument requires resolving some questions of interpretation. Is his rejection of political institutions merely a matter of transitional strategy, a way of getting from where we are now to the world envisioned in the two-track model, in which governing bodies implement the considered desires of civil society? Or is it a matter of principle, which signals a different end goal, a world without institutionalized public powers? Likewise, does he hold that formal political institutions merely *tend* to co-opt public opinion, all other things being equal? Or does he view that outcome as an ironclad necessity, entailed by the very nature of government as such?

As I see it, the stronger thesis, which takes as its end goal a democracy without formal political institutions, is conceptually incoherent. Premised on a single-track model of politics, this thesis purports to dispense with the distinction between civil-society publics and institutional actors. It assumes, accordingly, that a single body (the self-managed council) can play the part at once of both those instances. But this presupposes that everyone can always act collectively on everything that concerns them. Failing that absurd proposition, the question of accountability must arise: In what way and to what extent are a council's actions accountable to non-participants who are affected by or subjected to its decisions? These 'others' are, in effect, the council's public(s). From their perspective, moreover, the council itself is an institutionalized power, to be subjected to independent scrutiny and, when necessary, to contestation. *Qua* political actors, then, self-organized collectives do not circumvent the need for autonomous publics. But the converse is equally true. Far from being self-implementing, publics require institutionalized powers to effect their will. Counterpowers by definition, they lose their *raison d'être* in the absence of such powers, whose actions they seek to align with public opinion. The civil-society counterpart of formal political actors, informal publicity can never replace the latter, but must strive *ad infinitum* to guide and constrain them. In general, then, the distinction between publics and institutions is not so easily dispensed with. It returns, inevitably, to haunt Kurasawa's scenario. An anarchism that would simply scrap the two-track model is conceptually incoherent.

If anarchism is not viable as an end goal, how does it fare as a transitional strategy in the current conjuncture? Certainly, Kurasawa's affirmation of anti-systemic movements and subaltern counterpublics affords a salutary corrective to Couldry's faith in mainstream national media and to Nash's technocratic elitism. After all, it is only thanks to direct action by the independent militants associated with Occupy, WikiLeaks, and the World Social Forum that radical criticism has managed to pierce the veil of economistic and militaristic apologetics that dominates official public discourse in the present era. But anarchist tactics are not themselves sufficient to effect fundamental structural change. The strategy of evading, rather than confronting, the institutions of global governance lets off scot-free the mammoth concentrations of private power whose interests now rule. In fact, finance and corporate capital are the chief beneficiaries of efforts to retrench, let alone de-institutionalize, public authorities. It is better to fight to democratize, than to abolish, the institutions that regulate transnational interaction in a globalizing world. It is better, too, to adopt the account of subaltern counterpublics I proposed in 'Rethinking the Public Sphere', which counselled 'engaged withdrawal' not for the sake of any principled separatism, but as an agitational tactic, aimed at empowering subordinate voices in the battle for hearts and minds in wider publics. It is better, in sum, to treat direct action as one among several weapons in one's arsenal, and not as the master strategy for social change.

The larger lesson is 'don't throw out the baby with the bathwater'. Kurasawa is right that the process of translating public opinion into implementable policy can easily go awry – as, for example when emancipatory claims are rewritten as administrative regulations, and citizens are turned into clients, a process I analysed at the national level in a 1989 essay, 'Struggle over Needs'. But, as I argued there, translation should neither be equated with domination nor be eschewed altogether. The better course is to recognize the power of bureaucratizing tendencies and to envision counter-instances that work against them. That was the spirit in which I contemplated the possibility of 'hybrid strong publics' in 'Rethinking the Public Sphere' – a proposition exemplified in participatory budgeting and aimed not at collapsing the two tracks of the public-sphere model, but at softening the border that separates them, making them more porous to each other, and enhancing the flow of communication between them.

In that spirit, too, I conclude here that a critical theory of the public sphere should incorporate Kurasawa's best insights, while rejecting his wholesale anarchism. The latter perspective is implicitly vanguardist, I think, appealing chiefly to (especially male segments of) a precariat of relatively privileged but downwardly mobile youth, on the one hand, and to isolated indigenous communities struggling to subsist off the grid, on the other. Certainly, the view that representation is tantamount to domination is far too hyperbolic to tap the potential for broad-based emancipatory struggle in our situation. Like the scenarios envisioned by Nash and Couldry, albeit from the other, 'utopian' side, 'anarchist cosmopolitanism' fails to sustain the requisite tension between fact and norm.

A Postcolonial Challenge

Read together, the contributions by Couldry, Nash, and Kurasawa show how hard it is to reconstruct public-sphere theory under current conditions. Ostensibly aimed at remedying empirical lacunae in my diagnosis, their essays end up adjusting the normative bar – whether downwards, to a 'realism' that is beneath the level required for emancipatory change, or upwards, to an 'idealism' that flies over the heads of the social actors who would have to make it. As a result, none of these three respondents succeeds in striking the balance required by a critical theory. None locates here, in the present constellation, both norms of critique and motivations to act that point beyond it. None discloses the potential, immanent in our situation, for emancipatory social transformation.

But what if the trouble runs deeper? What if the difficulties we've encountered so far are symptomatic, indicative of historical impasses and conceptual blockages so intractable as to subvert the entire project? What if the current conjuncture harbours no emancipatory potential of the sort envisioned by a critical theory of the public sphere?

A variant of postcolonial critique raises just this possibility. In this view, public-sphere theory is premised upon the distinctive historical experience of modern subjects in the Global North. It is they, and they alone, who have undergone processes of democratization in territorial states that possessed the capacity to solve their problems and meet their needs. It is they, and they alone, who are suffering now from the loss of that capacity. It is they, and they alone, therefore, who could conceivably aspire to create an analogous framework on a broader scale – a transnational democratic framework within which legitimate public opinion can be mobilized across borders to constrain efficacious public power at the global level. Whatever confidence those subjects may have in that possibility cannot be generalized to non-European peoples with little experience of effective state sovereignty and even less basis for trust in global institutions. Public-sphere theory, so the argument goes, is Eurocentric. Instead of scaling it up in the current conjuncture, we should replace it with some other framework, better able to express the emancipatory hopes of postcolonial subjects in the Global South.

Kimberly Hutchings develops an argument of this sort. Broadening my effort to problematize the 'who' and 'how' of public-sphere theory, she proposes in addition to interrogate the 'when'. In historicizing my *Zeitdiagnose*, she claims, I told a before-and-after story about popular sovereignty originally won through democratization and subsequently lost through globalization. For Hutchings, this framing cannot undergird the reconstruction of public-sphere theory. Premised on 'first world' experiences not shared by postcolonial subjects, it runs afoul of a crucial, *temporal* presupposition of democratic publicity, a presupposition overlooked by me. A public sphere requires a specifically modern subjective standpoint, through which private individuals regard themselves as members of a public, free and equal. Also required is a modern temporal horizon, through which they orient themselves to the present as a problem. Indispensable as well are a shared social imaginary and historical narrative through which participants view themselves, not simply as jointly imbricated in the same causal nexus, but as engaged together in the common project of subjecting the conditions affecting their lives to collective control. As Hutchings sees it, these conditions do not obtain transnationally at the present time. For postcolonial subjects, twenty-first-century globalization is just the latest in a long series of predatory international arrangements, which never permitted effective control over their life-conditions by states of their own. A narrative frame that presents that state of affairs as historically new is ideological and morally obtuse. In the present context, where historical horizons diverge, we lack the requisite subjective basis for transnational publicity. Absent a social imaginary shared by the Global South and the Global North, the project of scaling up public-sphere theory is doomed to fail.

Here too I propose not to dwell on, but merely to mention, some interpretive lapses: that I never presented the Westphalian framing of public-sphere theory as a simple reflection of geopolitical reality; that I treated it, rather, as an imaginary construction – at odds with imperialist realities, but nevertheless hegemonic, performatively instated and materially consequential – hence able to shape the aspirations of most 'third world' movements for national liberation in the twentieth century; that I expressed my own doubts about the 'all-affected principle', whose objectivism is out of sync with the ideal of public autonomy so central to public-sphere theory; that soon thereafter I dropped that notion in favour of the 'all-subjected principle', which, I will argue below, is not open to Hutchings's objections.

Let me focus instead on Hutchings's important argument about the necessary subjective conditions for democratic publicity. She is right, I think, to insist on such conditions and to reject the view that mere 'affectedness' is a sufficient basis for people to recognize themselves as fellow members of a public. But I find her account of these matters problematic. The trouble is that she runs together what we might call 'formal' subjective conditions, which may indeed be necessary for democratic publicity, with shared substantive understandings, which are not. In the first category I include such general features of modern subjectivity as a disposition to regard the present situation as posing challenges requiring collective action to shape the future; a disposition to frame such challenges historically through narratives that connect past, present, and future; a disposition to regard oneself as a free and equal being whose views should count when it comes to deciding how to meet such challenges; and a disposition to resent subjection to arbitrary, unjustified power to which one has not been asked to consent. In my view, these formal subjective conditions are widely fulfilled today across the North/South divide. They underlay virtually all currents of the Arab Spring, from liberal to Islamist to leftist, and virtually all variants of anti-imperialism, from nationalist to Marxist to postcolonial. With respect to these formal subjective conditions, *we are all moderns now*, even though the paths by which we came to modernity are multiple, as are our modernities themselves.

The contents of subjectivity are another matter. In this category I include substantive interpretations of present challenges and desirable futures, as framed by substantive historical narratives relating past, present, and future in specific ways. Also included are substantive interpretations of freedom and equality and of what counts as unjustified power and proper consent. These interpretations, clearly, are not shared between Global North and Global South. But neither are they shared within those blocs, nor indeed within territorial states. Fortunately, agreement at this substantive level is not a necessary condition for democratic publicity. On the contrary, interpretive conflicts over matters like these are the very stuff and substance of public debate at every scale.

A telling example is today's transnational debate over global warming. On this issue, the Northern powers that industrialized early are proposing to tie a country's share of the burdens of remediation to its present-day levels of carbon emissions, while the BRICS nations (Brazil, Russia, India, China, and South Africa) and other late industrializers in the Global South insist that those who polluted the planet for two hundred years bear the lion's share of responsibility and should shoulder the lion's share of the costs. Engaged here in communicative contest are two perspectives that share the formal properties of modern subjectivity but diverge in historical framing and interpretive substance. Neither has difficulty recognizing the other as its partner-cum-antagonist in debate. Each finds in their common publicity the reflexive resources for thematizing their disagreements and waging the conflict. To be sure, the debate does not proceed ideally, in the way that public-sphere theory says it should. But the reason is neither the divergence of the parties' temporal horizons nor the unwillingness of Southerners to practise forms of publicity they deem Eurocentric. What derails publicity, here as elsewhere, is power asymmetry, the absence of participatory parity among the interlocutors. It is power asymmetry, too, that affords some the privilege of disregarding the views of others, ensuring that those most inclined to refuse transnational debate are not postcolonial subjects, but the citizens of the capitalist core.

Altogether, Hutchings's undeniably brilliant arguments do not persuade me that public-sphere theory cannot be reconstructed in the current conjuncture. She may be right that my previous essay failed to give adequate weight to the perspectives of postcolonial subjects. But the solution is not to abandon the critical theory of democratic publicity. It is rather to develop a more comprehensive *Zeitdiagnose* to motivate the theory. What is needed is a narrative frame that connects the historical experiences of postcolonials with those of their counterparts in the Global North. Such a frame should show both that the 'golden age' of the latter was built on the subjection of the former and also that the rise of the BRICS nations is intimately linked to the de-industrialization and financialization that have hollowed out democratic citizenship in the capitalist core. The story must capture the 'nonsynchronous synchronicity' (Bloch 1977) of both those horizons, as well as the internal complexity of each.

A *leitmotif* of any such story, it seems to me, will be the quintessentially modern disposition, mentioned earlier, to resent subjection to arbitrary, unjustified power to which one has not been asked to consent. Although the experience of such subjection may be more continuous for some than for others, I see no reason to doubt that it is deeply resented by all. If so, then the 'all-subjected principle' affords a possible basis for transnationalizing critical theory in the twenty-first century. The principle holds that all who are subjected to a given structure of governance, which sets the ground rules for their interaction, have political standing in relation to it. At one level, this is an objective question, to be sure. But unlike the objective condition of causal affectedness, subjection also carries a powerful subjective charge, a set of historical resonances that stamp the experience of it as offensive across the entire spectrum of multiple modernities. The palpable desire to overcome subjection, to elevate one's status 'from subject to citizen', lies behind contemporary political currents as diverse as anti-globalization, anarchism, postcolonialism, republicanism, democratic socialism, cosmopolitan democracy, and alter-globalization. A critical theory of the public sphere that invokes the all-subjected principle taps into that aspiration, which is immanent in, indeed formative for, the present situation. Appealing to *all* who experience subjection, albeit in different ways and according to different temporalities, such a theory discloses the basis for subaltern counterpublicity on a transnational scale. Perhaps it could also facilitate formation of a counter-hegemonic bloc that seeks an emancipatory transformation of global society.

Further Philosophical Reflections

To this point, I have stressed the stringent constraints that a critical theory of the public sphere must observe in the present era. I have emphasized that such a theory must ground its norms immanently, in historically sedimented understandings and motivations that are potentially available to social actors across state borders. At the same time, I have insisted that the norms in question must point beyond the present context, to a successor society that resolves our current impasses in an emancipatory way. Threading this needle is far from easy, to be sure. But I have suggested that a theory centred on the all-subjected principle could fit the bill. Let me elaborate.

The notion that everyone who is subjected to a given governance structure should have political standing in relation to it points to an expanded understanding of public-sphere theory's central ideal of public autonomy. In this view, entitlement to participate in collective opinion and will formation is not restricted to citizenship in bounded territorial states, although it includes that, to be sure. Such participation is also required in relation to non-state structures of governance, at both smaller and larger scales. Of special pertinence to our discussion are the structures of global governance discussed by Kate Nash. If we apply the principle to institutions such as the International Monetary Fund, the International Atomic Energy Agency, and the Agreement on

Trade-Related Aspects of Intellectual Property Rights, then
we conclude that whoever is subject to their regulations is
entitled to participate in collective processes of opinion and
will formation concerning the matters they regulate, regardless of formal citizenship. How precisely such participation
is organized remains to be seen. Minimally, the transnational community of those subjected comprises a transnational public, charged with bringing the decision-makers to
account informally, in civil society. Maximally, that community could also comprise a transnational *demos*, with
formal voting rights in global governance institutions. In
either case, the idea that subjection confers a right to participation serves to broaden the scope of democratic publicity
beyond state borders. The results could mitigate, if not overcome, our current mismatches of scale among public spheres,
private powers, and political institutions.

But does the all-subjected principle really provide an adequate basis for a critical theory of democratic publicity
under current conditions? Is it really sufficient for envision-
ing new arrangements in which transnational public opinion
is legitimately generated and efficaciously mobilized to
disable concentrations of private power and regulate common
affairs in the interest of all? Does the principle really indicate
a path to an emancipatory social transformation?

David Owen has some doubts. Bringing an acute philo-
sophical intelligence to bear on these questions, he contends
that the all-subjected principle is vulnerable to two objections. First, the principle is triggered, by definition, only in
circumstances where social interaction is already regulated
by a governance structure; where no such structure exists,
it does not apply. Thus, it gains no critical traction in
what we might call the 'wild zones' of globalization, those
Hobbesian spaces where private powers impose their will
with total impunity, unimpeded by any pretence of regulation. Efforts to counter domination in those spaces find no
support in a principle aimed at democratizing institutions of
governance that already exist. Such efforts require another

principle, one that justifies pacifying the state of nature, establishing *new* institutions charged with regulating hitherto unregulated zones or aspects of social interaction.

Second, the subjection criterion confers participation rights only on persons whose interactions with one another fall directly under the regulatory jurisdiction of a governance structure; those not subject to the structure's rules land outside the circle of those with political standing. This means that persons affected by, but not directly subject to, say, the protocols of the International Monetary Fund cannot justifiably claim a say with respect to the Fund's operations. That result is counterintuitive, however, when their fundamental, life-and-death interests may be at stake. If we assume that such persons, too, deserve to be heard, then we will need to turn elsewhere, to some other normative principle, to justify their inclusion in the ranks of participants. The all-subjected principle does not avail.

For Owen, the solution is to develop a dual approach. In cases where the all-subjected principle applies, critical theorists should invoke it. Where it does not apply, they should turn instead to the all-affected principle, which serves as a supplement to fill in the gaps. Thus, when the question is whether to establish new structures of governance in wild zones, everyone potentially *affected* should have a say. When the issue is holding accountable an existing governance structure, by contrast, all *subjected* deserve a voice. But even here, in the second case, affectedness should play a role, in Owen's view. As he sees it, such situations encompass two distinct interests in participation, which need to be given expression in two distinct publics. In one public, call it 'ordinary political', those who are directly subject to a structure's regulations should have a voice in collective communication aimed at holding the decision-makers to account. In a second public, call it 'metapolitical', all affected (whether subject or not) should have a say in determining whether the structure's decisions should be subject to regulation by a higher-level structure of governance.[2] Both publics, the ordinary political and the metapolitical, enjoy political standing in this account. But the character of that standing and the rationale for it differ. Ordinary-political publics have a participation interest grounded in direct subjection, while metapolitical publics have one grounded in causal affected-ness. Presumably, the first, subjection-based interest is stronger than the second. But both interests must be given their due. Both notions – subjection and affectedness – deserve a place in a critical theory of democratic publicity for the present era.

Owen's proposal is as ingenious as his analysis is perspicacious. He is right, I think, to stress that the all-subjected principle does not justify efforts to pacify wild zones. But in order to determine how serious this limitation is, we must figure out whether and to what extent such wild zones exist. Owen notes that the all-subjected principle would work just fine if it were the case that 'the polities of, structures of governance of, and relations between these governmental entities that compose the contemporary global political order can themselves be seen as comprising a regime of global governance'. In that case,

> those whose interests are affected in morally significant ways by the decisions of any given structure of governance but who are not themselves part of this particular structure of governance have, on the basis of their subjection to the regime of global governance, an entitlement to inclusion within a global public in which the moral costs and political legitimacy of this current global ordering of governance can be addressed. (p. 124)

In this view, everyone is subject to the overarching regime of global governance, no wild zones exist, and recourse to the all-affected principle is unnecessary.

Is this a plausible picture of our situation? Is our problem that we lack an overarching global governance regime and need to build one? Or is it that we have one but lack the means to hold it accountable? Certainly, this question is not so easy to answer, implicating as it does a host of difficult issues of social theory and historical interpretation; and I cannot pretend to resolve it definitely here. Nevertheless, I incline to the view that there does exist an overarching regime of global governance to which everyone is subject. The key components of this regime are, first, a capitalist world system founded on private property rights and organized for the sake of limitless accumulation and private appropriation of surplus; and, second, an interstate system that was originally and officially premised on mutual recognition of equal sovereign states, even as that idea was belied in fact both by (post)colonial power asymmetries and by the geopolitical hegemony of Great Powers, a system that is now in any case mutating, increasingly overlaid by a growing body of international law, on the one hand, and by a motley mix of nonstate governance institutions – interstate, transnational, global – on the other hand. Exactly how these regime components intersect remains to be specified. One need not (indeed probably should not) assume that they fit together in ways that are logically neat and practically frictionless. Nor need one assume that there exist no gaps – no failed states, civil wars, or lawless zones; no matters of common concern that cry out for wholly new or vastly improved regulation. Such gaps do exist, of course, but at lower levels, beneath the overarching regime. Thus, they do not contravene the idea of a global governance regime at the highest level, a regime that spans the whole of political space and sets the parameters for institutionalization at lower levels. But if that is right, then there already exists 'in-itself', if not yet 'for-itself', the basis for a global public sphere of all subjected.

This picture, if plausible, allows us to deal simultaneously with both of Owen's objections. First, it resituates wild zones as local spaces within a world already subjected to an overarching global governance regime; as a result, it enables us to justify broad-based participation in decision-making as to whether to regulate those zones by appeal to such subjection. Second, the picture I just sketched allows us to reinterpret

Owen's two publics as premised on two different levels of subjection, one to the 'local' governance structure, the other to the overarching regime; thus, participation rights in both publics, the ordinary political and the metapolitical, can be justified in terms of subjection. In neither case, therefore, is appeal to affectedness needed. The all-subjected principle alone suffices.

In general, then, my inclination is to bite the bullet and stick with the all-subjected principle as the master norm for determining the 'who' of public-sphere theory. Granted, this requires me to shoulder the admittedly difficult burden of arguing for an overarching global regime. But the advantages seem to me to outweigh the trouble. Subjection, unlike affectedness, is a powerful term, laden with offensive connotations, deeply engrained in modern history, and resonant for populations across the globe. Far more than affectedness, therefore, it has the potential to satisfy the twin requirements for a critical theory: first, that the theory's norms be immanent in our situation and broadly available to potential actors; and, second, that they point beyond that situation, to an emancipatory overcoming of its characteristic forms of domination.

Conclusion

Each of the five contributors to this volume raises important questions about the prospects for reimagining the critical theory of democratic publicity in a form adequate to our time. Politically, they cover virtually the entire spectrum of possibilities, from democratic nationalism to elite transnational governance, from anarchist cosmopolitanism to postcolonial critique. Methodologically, they draw on a broad range of orientations – media studies and political sociology, social movement theory and philosophy of history, political theory and moral philosophy. Conceptually, they introduce a slew of fruitful new ideas for thinking about publicity: a distinction between a transnationalized public sphere and a transnational one; a proposal for enriching the theory's normative base with ideals drawn from contemporary practices; an identification of counter-systemic movements oriented to direct action as the leading edge of transnational publicity in our time; a concept of publicity's subjective conditions, especially the relevance of historical and temporal horizons; and a strategy for assessing the strengths and limitations of the all-subjected principle.

Taken together, the contributors' essays testify to the continuing vitality and importance of public-sphere theory. That theory has a rich history, descending at least from Kant. The present volume leads me to think it will continue to prove fertile in the future. The reason, I think, has to do with the theory's central idea, which inspires all the contributors, including me: that ordinary people are not just objects of the designs of the great, but political subjects; that they deserve a decisive say in the matters that concern them in common; that they have the capacity to mobilize communicative power both as a means to effect change and as an end in itself. Despite our differences, all of us subscribe to that proposition and hope that our discussion will serve to advance it.

Notes

1 I am grateful to Jannik Pfister and Wu Yun-Chan for helpful discussions of these materials.
2 I am here adapting terminology I used to distinguish two different levels of political injustice in my 'Reframing Justice in a Global World' (Fraser 2008).

References

Bloch, E. (1977) 'Nonsynchronism and the Obligation to Its Dialectics', *New German Critique* 11: 22–38.
Fraser, N. (1989) 'Struggle over Needs: Outline of a Socialist-Feminist Critical Theory of Late-Capitalist Political Culture',

in *Unruly Practices: Power, Discourse and Gender in Contemporary Social Theory*. Cambridge: Polity.

Fraser, N. (1992) 'Rethinking the Public Sphere: A Contribution to the Critique of Actually Existing Democracy', in C. Calhoun (ed.), *Habermas and the Public Sphere*. Cambridge, MA: MIT Press, 1992.

Fraser, N. (2008) 'Reframing Justice in a Globalizing World', in *Scales of Justice: Reimaging Political Space in a Globalizing World*. Cambridge: Polity.

Index

CPSIA information can be obtained
at www.ICGtesting.com
Printed in the USA
JSHW030946141222
34804JS00006B/198